Dive

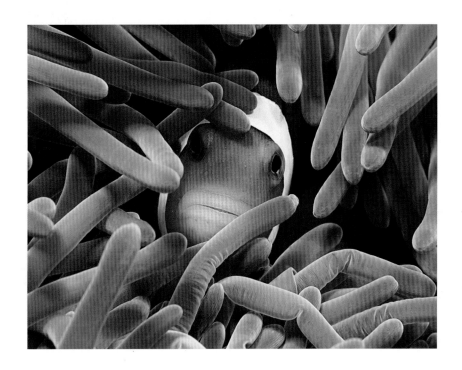

Dive

The World's Best Dive Destinations

Lawson Wood

Quercus

184 Vancouver Island

80 Newfoundland

88 Scapa Flow

54 Florida

92 St Abbs and Eyemouth

24 Isla Mujeres, Mexico

98 Cornwall

96 Farne Islands

60 Bahamas

20 Yucatán, Mexico

108 Cyprus

76 Bermuda

84 Azores

66 Turks and Caicos

180 Channel Islands

100 Medas Islands

42 St Lucia

176 Baja California

38 Tobago

104 Malta, Gozo and Comino

170 Golden Triangle, Galápagos

112 Northern Red Sea

46 Dominica

26 Belize

50 British Virgin Islands

30 Bay Islands, Honduras

34 Dutch Antilles

72 Brazil

10 Cuba

122 Seychelles

14 Cayman Islands

126 South Africa

Contents

148 Pacific Islands

154 Micronesia

130 Malaysia

142 Eastern Indonesia

134 Western Indonesia

118 Maldives

160 French Polynesia

164 Eastern Australia

168 New Zealand

Introduction

Compiling a book about the world's best dive sites is a daunting task when you consider just how many millions of hours that divers spend underwater each year in every ocean and sea in every part of the world. No longer are climate zones, depth, or water temperature a problem as a result of the very latest scuba-diving equipment and the high quality of training available through professional diving agencies, such as PADI, BSAC, SSAC, NAUII, and CMAS. Training and expertise once only available to the most professional of divers is now offered to everyone. For the first time many shipwrecks, deep submerged reefs, and underground cave systems can be explored, adding hugely to our knowledge of our underwater world.

When assessing the world's best dive sites you must remember that old adage: location, location, location. Areas where diving is very popular depend on a professional infrastructure encompassing accommodation, professional dive companies, live-aboard dive boats, ease of travel, relative cost, the seriousness of the diving, excellent chances for photography, and whether the diving can be a part of a wider vacation experience that could, for instance, be enjoyed by the whole family. Scuba (Self-Contained Underwater Breathing Apparatus) can be practiced from the age of 11 onward. Indeed there is no ageism or social discrimination in this sport: it is there for anyone who wants to explore our underwater world, whether through scuba diving, technical diving, or snorkeling. The desire to be in, on, or under the sea is the primary motivation. Discovering species of marine creature that you have never seen before, researching a historic shipwreck, swimming with some of the largest creatures on the planet, or just snorkeling along the edge of a precipitous coral wall puts the rest of our terrestrial world into a better perspective. I recently spent the time of my life in only 20ft (6m) of water swimming with and photographing great hammerhead sharks in Bimini, the Bahamas.

Some divers are lucky enough to live in close proximity to the sea, a scenic river, lake, or flooded quarry, but for everyone else some travel will be involved, often to largely uninhabited regions of the globe where small specialist companies promote, protect, and take care of some of the most diverse areas sustaining marine life on the planet. Places like Raja Ampat in New Guinea where the greatest number of marine species ever recorded are found in one small zone, or Manado in North Sulawesi where the house reef at Tasik Ria is home to the most fish species found anywhere on the planet. It is important to mention these two sites, as they are at the heart of the ancient lost supercontinent of Pangaea. Over millions of years, our land masses have moved around on the face of the planet by the action of continental drift driven by the active tectonic plates of the planet. The Indo/Pacific zone is recognized as the "hub" of species diversity on the planet—all other marine species are adaptations of those that first evolved in this primordial swamp.

The choice of dive sites included in this volume is based on my personal experience and knowledge of our oceans. As an underwater photographer, when I rate a site, it is not only for the ease of obtaining great photographs, it is also for the undiluted thrill of experiencing once-in-a-lifetime moments. Underwater photography is not straightforward: the diver is moving, the element of the water is moving, the subject is moving, in general you are working in an extremely corrosive and salty environment and both mentally and physically under pressure, with only a limited time in only a shallow range of depths to obtain your photographs. Thousands of other dives might have been included in the book, but it has been conceived as a guide to whet your appetite, before you immerse yourself in exploring our underwater world further. It gives you a starting point and I hope will encourage you to explore other regions and enjoy the experience of life-defining moments in the company of the greatest variety of creatures on Earth.

OPPOSITE: More than anything, we should have fun while pursuing our passion underwater and always dive safely.

Caribbean Sea, Florida, and the Gulf Islands

Cuba

Caribbean Sea

By far the largest island nation in the Caribbean, Cuba hosts the second largest barrier reef in the Caribbean and the third largest in the world. A total absence of diver pollution and scant commercial fishing or shoreline development have resulted in probably the most pristine coral reefs in the entire region. There are numerous diving locations around the island, but invariably you require a live-aboard dive boat and plenty of time to give the reefs the proper attention they deserve.

Still estranged from the United States after the coup led by Fidel Castro in 1959, the island covers around 43,000sq miles (111,000km²) and is located due south of Florida. Indeed when flying south to visit the Cayman Islands or Honduras, you will fly over Cuba and can marvel as the colors of the water change from light aquamarine shades in the shallows to the deep indigo blue of the depths. Tantalizing shallow seamounts and pinnacles can be seen and you know that the diving will be exceptional. The island has now opened itself up to mass tourism and is considered the number one vacation location in the Caribbean, but scuba diving is still in its infancy.

With the Caribbean Sea to the south and the Gulf of Mexico to the north, the Gulf Stream passes along the western seaboard of Cuba before it heads east through the Florida Keys and the Bahamas and then flowing past Bermuda. The southwest and west coast of the island and in particular the areas around **Cayo Largo**, **Isla de la Juventud** (the Isle of Youth), and **Maria La Gorda** are all exceptional with very good corals and sponges, schools of fish, great chances to encounter large pelagic fish, and vertical walls that just beckon you a little further.

The thin string of low-lying islands to the east of the Isle of Youth and west of **Los Jardines de la Reina** (the Gardens of the Queen) reveal a remarkable number of canyons and fissures that traverse the reef. Over 30 mooring buoys have been placed along the coral lip where massive barrel sponges, Nassau grouper, blue chromis, and schools of horse-eye jacks vie for your attention. Huge sand chutes plunge into

RIGHT: The invasive lionfish, originally from the Indo-Pacific region is now widespread throughout the Caribbean and Bermuda. Released accidentally into the ocean, it has very few natural predators to control its numbers.
BELOW: The coral buttresses of Maria la Gorda are covered in colorful sponges and sea fans.

the depths creating mini-walls perfect for exploration at any depth. The Isle of Youth is protected by a barrier reef that runs along Cuba's southern coast and here the reef wall comes very close to the shore. Huge canyons cut the reef where silverside minnows are chased by schools of tarpon. Lionfish are also very common here and since there is little diving done, there has been an explosion of these tropical interlopers. Thankfully the local grouper population have cottoned onto the fact that these fish are also quite tasty and will feed on them.

Cueva Azul, El Pasaje Escondido, El Salto, Piedra de Coral, and Pequeno Reino are all worth mentioning, but they just scratch the surface of what is available. These coral reefs are generally undercut and have numerous caves and caverns where lobsters and large channel-clinging crabs are found. At night tiny red shrimp with iridescent green eyes wink at you and there are lots of octopuses along this reef edge, quite often changing to an amazing aquamarine blue color while feeding on small crustaceans and fish. Sleeping parrotfish can be seen hiding in their mucus membrane cocoons and if you listen closely, you can hear the rhythmic grunting of the toadfish which hide under coral overhangs. Hermit crabs covered in symbiotic anemones scavenge the sandy seabed for tidbits, while large tarpon patrol the reef walls.

Maria La Gorda

Maria La Gorda is a protected area and although a long drive from Havana, the trip is well worth the effort as it passes through some of Cuba's most amazing scenery and tobacco farms. However, you need to watch out for the insect life. Around dusk, little biting sand fleas can be brutal, so stay indoors until dark has fully arrived. There are a couple of piers where you catch the dive boats for just a short ride out to the wall which is swept by the Gulf Stream. Expect to do some drift diving here, but the huge coral buttresses always offer shelter.

More than 50 dive sites are buoyed here, and there is a wide selection of historic and modern shipwrecks, anchors, reefs, wall, gullies, canyons, and even a blue hole to explore. Sites such as Paraiso Perdido, Ancla del Pirata, and Las Tetas de Maria are all individually interesting, yet completely different, ranging from a buttress reef cut by sand chutes to a shallow reef and mini-wall, onto two massive coral bommies with near vertical sides, sometimes undercut and with a sand chute between them. Caribbean reef sharks, bull sharks, stingrays, and eagle rays are all commonly seen here and you should expect hawksbill turtles and large schools of fusilier and chromis.

OPPOSITE: Schools of horse-eye jacks cruise the coral canyons and in some areas where there is an upwelling of cooler water, many hundreds will collect in the same place.

Fact file Cuba

BEST TIME TO GO
Hurricane season is June through to November, but generally the Maria La Gorda area is relatively sheltered from any bad weather conditions or rough seas. It is great to dive at any time of the year, but it can be particularly hot during July and August.

UNDERWATER VISIBILITY AND TEMPERATURE
Visibility is usually more than 100ft (30m) and sea temperatures very rarely drop below 78°F (26°C) because of the influence of that huge sea engine, the Gulf Stream. Full wet suits are recommended because of the stinging things in the water, but generally you will be comfortable no matter what your diving skill or equipment. Expect to do deep diving, but enjoy the shallower reefs on the way back up.

THE BAHAMAS
La Habana   Matanzas   CUBA
Pinar del Río   Santa Clara
Cienfuegos   Ciego de Avila   Camagüey
Maria La Gorda   Isla de la Juventud   Cayo Largo   Holguín
Los Jardines de la Reina   Bayamo   Guantánamo
Cayman Islands (UK)   Santiago de Cuba
Montego Bay   Jérémie
Gulf of Mexico   Kingston   HAITI
0   200 km
0   100 miles   JAMAICA

Cayman Islands

Central Caribbean Sea

First visited by Christopher Columbus in 1503, his reports tell of incredible numbers of fish, turtles, and crocodiles. The latter gave rise to the original name of Caimen or the Cayman Islands. This British Crown Colony is located south of Cuba in the central Caribbean and consists principally of three islands: Grand Cayman, where the capital George Town and the main airport are found, Little Cayman Island, and Cayman Brac. There are some 300 shipwrecks recorded in these waters, testimony to their importance and strategic position in the Caribbean.

Grand Cayman

The Cayman Islands have some of the clearest waters in the Caribbean, with very few currents—they are the ideal destination for virtually guaranteed results. The group of islands sit atop three huge submarine mountains and incredibly deep water lies all around. Grand Cayman is the largest of the three islands at around 22 miles (35km) long. There is a superb fringing reef all along its north shore, fantastic historic wrecks at the east end, and now the *Kittiwake*, a decommissioned US Navy ship sunk as a dive

attraction. But the island is perhaps best known for its world-famous shallow dive and snorkel with wild stingrays. Known as Stingray City and the Sandbar, these two locations offer two distinctly different and fascinating stingray encounters.

The site known as **The Sandbar** is just that—a shallow sandbar approximately 3ft (1m) deep—and this is where most tourists are introduced to these splendid creatures. Handlers take in small pieces of squid and hand-feed the rays, bringing them directly to the tourists who can touch them. This location inside the protective barrier reef of North Sound is extremely popular with cruise ship passengers and hundreds of people may be on this site daily.

The deeper **Stingray City** offers the better encounter as this is in 10–17ft (3–5m) of water. Fewer visitors come to this site and while you can snorkel, it is better to scuba dive as you can get down beside the rays and observe their behavior more closely. Baiting still does occur here to get the best interaction between divers and fish, but it appears less frenzied and is certainly more peaceful without the hundreds of tourists.

Much maligned, the southern stingray (*Dasyatis americana*) is the most common of all the rays found in the Caribbean and Gulf Islands zone. Larger adults, some over 5ft (1.5m) in length, swoop in to take the bait from the outstretched hand of the dive master; smaller stingrays scoot around trying to steal food scraps and the feeling is one of pure excitement. Despite the melee and obvious entertainment value, as soon as the dive master stops feeding the rays, they return to their normal foraging pattern and ignore the divers. This still gives photographers plenty of

LEFT: The *Kittiwake* was sunk along Seven Mile Beach as a diver attraction in January 2011. Protected by a small buttress reef and lying virtually upright, it is a superb dive.
OPPOSITE: Large southern stingrays swoop in looking for tasty tidbits and are used to being handled by divers. They revert to their normal feeding behavior when the hand-feeding stops.

"... simply nothing can prepare you for that rush of adrenaline when you first see the rays."

opportunities to take great photographs, as quite often small nurse sharks and even large green moray eels will also take part in the show.

Stingray City and the Sandbar on Grand Cayman Island are amazing, and simply nothing can prepare you for that rush of adrenaline when you first see the rays. Suffice to say that several hundred thousand tourists have enjoyed the delights of interacting with one of nature's most amazing creatures and will continue to do so for many years to come.

Little Cayman

Over on Little Cayman, Jacques Yves Cousteau called **Bloody Bay Wall** one of the top ten dive sites in the world. The island itself is just 9 miles (14.5km) long and only has a handful of local residents. There are not many dive resorts and predictably these get very busy. But you only need to take a short walk to the end of the dock, jump aboard for a short boat ride, and you will be in some of the clearest waters you will ever see. The wall starts on some dive sites in very shallow waters with swimthroughs, sandy bowls where Pederson's shrimp can easily be found, while rays forage through the sand giving photographers the ideal opportunity for a close-up shot. The dramatic drop of Bloody Bay Wall is one of the most memorable sites in the world, not just for the color of sponges, sea fans, fish, and sea squirts, but also because the blue of the deeper water leaves an indelible memory. These are some of the most fantastic underwater vistas that have ever been photographed.

A number of the sites, particularly around the midway point at **Mixing Bowl**, are well known now for the fun that you can have with very large Nassau grouper (*Epinephelus striatus*). These have become extremely accustomed to divers feeding them lionfish—although this practice is sometimes frowned upon as it is the policy in the Cayman Islands to try to eradicate this interloper. The grouper will come right up to you which makes for some great photographic opportunities. To the east of Bloody Bay in the area known as **Jackson's Bight** are numerous massive caverns with sand chutes running from the sheltered inner lagoon in about 40ft (12m) of water right through to the outer wall in around 100ft (30m) and more. These make for an exciting introduction to the outer wall where Caribbean reef sharks are commonly seen, as are turtles, barracuda, and plenty of snapper and grunt.

Cayman Brac

Just 6 miles (10km) to the east of Little Cayman is Cayman Brac, an easily navigated island that is approximately 11 miles (18km) long by 1 mile (1.6km) wide. Not many divers are aware of this, but Cayman Brac offers the most shore dives of all three islands, with easy access and safe waters. In fact under a new initiative, Cayman Brac actually can offer more shore dives than any other Caribbean island. This is one of the best places to dive in the Caribbean.

OPPOSITE: During the summer months the coral caverns become home to millions of silverside minnows creating a moving wall of fish that can completely surround the diver.

Fact file Cayman Islands

BEST TIME TO GO
With air temperatures averaging 80–90°F (27–32°C) in the summer, it can be hot and humid and as always in the Caribbean, hurricane season is from June to November each year. However some of the best diving is also done in these same months as the sea is generally at its most calm, there are fewer tourists and better opportunities for marine life encounters. You can dive all year round, as all three Cayman Islands have great dive sites that are always available depending on the prevailing wind and weather.

UNDERWATER VISIBILITY AND TEMPERATURE
One point to emphasize here is that the underwater visibility is very rarely less that 100ft (30m). The temperature ranges from around 72°F (22°C) in December to 84°F (29°C) in July.

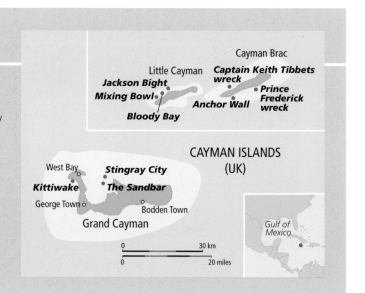

OPPOSITE: Large, friendly Nassau grouper are synonymous with Bloody Bay Wall on Little Cayman Island, where they patrol the reef drop-off looking for soldierfish and lionfish.

BELOW: Hawksbill turtles are very common around all three islands and divers will encounter them on most dives, particularly the friendly juveniles, like this.

Along the northwest shore can be found the wreck of the Russian Brigadier Type II Class frigate No. 356, renamed the *Captain Keith Tibbetts* after one of the island's notable men. This is a must-do dive. It can be reached from the shore but is better tackled as a boat dive from one of the dive resorts as it lies a fair distance from the shore. **Charlie's Reef** is another

shore dive that can easily be accessed. Leave your vehicle on the concrete dock at Scott's Pier and enter the water either by a foolhardy leap, or a more sedate descent down the stainless steel steps. The wall here starts fairly close to shore and while many people are quite content to spend their time among the excellent spur and groove reef formations, some opt for the longer swim out to the wall where there is a better chance to see large jacks, eagle rays, and sharks. All the way along the north shore are little red marker stones to indicate where the best shore dives are, but this encompasses perhaps only a third of the available access. The best is Burt Brothers opposite a small store called NiM Things (Native Island Made). A concrete boat ramp is great for access and it is just a short swim to some massive coral structures edged with deep-water gorgonians and their usual spider crabs. Hammerhead sharks are seen here in January and February, but really it is the fine colorful corals which make this dive special.

On the south shore, when the sea is calm, the wreck of the **Prince Frederick** which sank in 1897 can be reached from the shore. It is situated about halfway down the coastline and is easily identified as it lies directly out from a curiously shaped building known as the "Bubble House." It offers a shallow dive

with easy view of the remains of the ship. A handful of superb Trotman anchors, a steel mast, an anchor winch, ribs, hooks, and knees are all identifiable with good coral growth and many varieties of fish.

There are dive sites up and down the north and south shore of Cayman Brac, where rental vehicles can be left quite safely. Further down the south shore of Cayman Brac, if the sea is flat calm, the dive boats sometimes take guests down to the east end of the island for a rare but magnificent dive underneath the massive towering cliff known as **The Bluff**. At over 140ft (42m) high, it is the highest point by far in the Cayman Islands. This dive has to be done if you possibly can. Dramatic boulders and small pieces of an ancient wreck called the *Union* lie under the very tip of the east end of the island. It is easy to see why there is wreckage here because when you look up from underwater, you see the impressive drop of cliff into the deep water.

Both Cayman Brac and Little Cayman are reached by regular daily air service, with the jet service running to Cayman Brac twice a day on four days of the week. All three islands offer warm breezes and cold beers after a good day's diving for divers of all levels of experience. The lack of diver pollution guarantees quiet reefs and great quality corals.

Yucatán, Mexico

Western Caribbean Sea

Situated 65 miles (115km) southwest of Cuba and bordering Belize in the western Caribbean Sea, the Yucatán peninsula is an ancient limestone plateau that once stood more than 150ft (45m) above sea level. Its interior is honeycombed with blue holes, caves, and caverns similar to those that are found throughout the Caribbean. Here they are linked underwater for hundreds of miles. Known as cenoté, these natural aquifers were considered to be sacred by the Mayan Indians, who built their vast empire along these shores. The name cenoté is a Spanish corruption of the Mayan word tzenot. The great Mayan cities were all built around cenoté and the Mayans revered them deeply, offering gifts and sacrifices to their rain god Chac.

The area is entirely flat and when you climb up to the top of one of the breathtaking monuments at Coba or Chichén Itza, you can see distant "hills" all around. These hills are actually other ancient monuments and citadels. Only about 10% of the ruins have been discovered here and, of those, only 10% have been explored and documented archaeologically. The Yucatán is also thought to be the region where the giant asteroid that scientists believe was responsible for the extinction of the dinosaurs struck the Earth. The name Yucatán is something of a misnomer; when the Spanish conquistadors landed on the peninsula in 1530, they asked the locals what the area was called. They answered *"yucatán,"* which in the Mayan dialect means *"We do not understand you."* The name has stuck ever since. Now the invaders are tourists and the purpose-built resort of Cancún is a typical urban sprawl of hotels, malls, and tourist traps. Quite a lot of diving goes on here—principally out in the channel between the mainland and the two islands of **Isla Contoy** and **Isla Mujeres**. These long, low reefs have surprisingly large schools of fish and due to the constant movement of water here, virtually all of the dives are drift dives. Although the limestone reefs are predominantly covered in sponges, there are very good soft corals and colorful hard corals. The splendid toadfish (*Sanopus splendidus*) is found here, and its presence can be detected by listening out for its "croak" during night dives.

Mayan Riviera

To the south of Cancún lies the region referred to as the Mayan Riviera. Large numbers of hotels and tourist resorts have been constructed here, including golf courses and water parks. The architects tend to incorporate ancient ruins within these complexes, as there are just so many of them. There are also specific ancient sites, such as Tulum, where one of the stone carvings is said to represent a "diving" god! Toward Akumal around 60 miles (100km) south of Cancún is where you are able to start exploring the many cenoté which are open to the public.

There are literally thousands of these openings, all of which are interconnected to some degree or another. Many miles of explored passages have been marked and laid with exploration lines, but for the most part regular sports divers are able to look around the entrances to many of these caverns without the need for specialized training. Around 50

LEFT: Colorful peppermint gobies with their yellow bodies and distinctive large blue eyes can be found perched on the various hard corals.

of the *cenoté* are found along the Akumal/Tulum Corridor south of Cancún. They are now well mapped, but still not completely explored. There are no other places on Earth that can compare with this. All of the *cenoté* diving takes place on private land. Some have crude changing huts or simple platforms at the water's edge, but not all do. You will be expected to pay a fee to the land owner for access.

Sites such as **Car Wash**, **Ponderosa**, **Dos Ojo**, and **Gran Cenoté** (also known as El Grande Cenoté) are superb and really give you an idea of the scale and majesty of these ancient caverns. El Grande Cenoté is a massive circular collapsed cavern measuring more than 200ft (60m) across. Most of it is filled

ABOVE: Deepwater gorgonian sea fans stretch out into the current to snare plankton and act as holdfasts for spider crabs and crinoids.

are interconnecting is a recent discovery and much of this subterranean landscape is still unexplored.

Over on the nearby island of Cozumel, the diving is virtually all drift diving along the western coastline of this 29-mile (47-km) long island. A tail of the Gulf Stream pushes up between Cozumel and the Mexican coastline. It always runs north, so your drift dive may begin at one dive site and end up at another. **Palancar Reef** is highly regarded by divers: it is a massive site with a mini-wall in about 50ft (15m), followed by a large patch reef system which turns into a large coral buttress wall that is indented and cut by hundreds of fissures and canyons. This reef is 3 miles (5km) long and has enough variety and range of depths to suit all levels of diver.

The predominant reef life consists of multitudes of brightly colored sponges, interspersed with patches of bright green algae. Fed by this nutrient-rich current, the sponges grow to be spectacular. Soft and hard coral growth is also very good, but it is the sponges that stand out. There isn't as much fish life here as on other Caribbean reefs, but the grandeur of the walls more than make up for this deficiency. When conditions are right to dive on the east coast, there are curiously shaped, small coral bommies, and of course, a better chance to see plenty of sharks.

with rubble, but to the left of the steps is an entrance covered with lilies that leads into the crystal clear interior. With visibility of at least 200ft (60m), you can see a tiny pinprick of light away in the distance where another *cenoté* is revealed. The entrance to Car Wash is a lot less impressive; set amidst a tumble of trees and branches, you lower yourself into a small pond with annoying, biting little fish. Once inside, however, the greenish tinge to the water takes on a clear blue quality. The fact that many of these wells and caverns

Fact file **Yucatán, Mexico**

BEST TIME TO GO
The region is tropical maritime in climate with a very high humidity and summer temperatures that can easily reach 104°F (40°C). Hurricane season is June to November, but usually storms come later in the year and may be influenced by the Pacific. November to March is best for the *cenoté* and May to September are the best months for Cozumel and Cancún.

UNDERWATER VISIBILITY AND TEMPERATURE
Visibility is always exceptional. It is well over 100ft (30m) on the outer reefs and "gin clear" in the *cenoté*. The temperature generally stays at around 82°F (28°C) due to the constant push of the Gulf Stream.

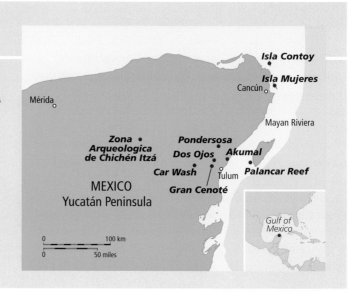

Isla Contoy
Isla Mujeres
Cancún
Mérida
Mayan Riviera
Zona Arqueologica de Chichén Itzá
Pondersosa
Dos Ojos
Akumal
Car Wash
Tulum
Palancar Reef
MEXICO
Yucatán Peninsula
Gran Cenoté
Gulf of Mexico
0 ___ 100 km
0 ___ 50 miles

Isla Mujeres, Mexico

Western Caribbean Sea

One of the new experiences that has recently grabbed divers' attention is hunting out the migrating schools of Brazilian sardines that pass up through the Gulf Stream to the waters around Isla Mujeres, just north of the resort of Cancún on Mexico's Yucatán Peninsula. This is an expensive and demanding trip and only those with great patience and swimming endurance should take it on. Accommodation is provided on shore at either Isla Mujeres or Cancún, and boats usually leave around j6 a.m. to venture out north of Isla Mujeres, perhaps as far as 30–60 miles (50–100km) away.

January to March are the best months and you must give yourself plenty of time to maximize your chances, so February is probably best for sightings. Even then, you can spend several days not getting a sighting or perhaps just a brief encounter. On other trips you may enjoy more than 40 minutes of action while a full-blown attack is going on. Numbers are limited to only four or five divers in the water to get the best conditions and to avoid getting in each other's way. But you really are in the lap of the ancient Mayan Gods with regards to this sometimes exhilarating (or sometimes extremely boring) trip.

It is rather like the sardine run in South Africa, but here the emphasis is on observing the huge Atlantic sailfish (*Istiophorus albicans*). The sardines form tightly packed "baitballs" for protection when they come under attack as the predatory sailfish home in on them. The huge numbers of sardines that pass through these waters create a lot of underwater "noise" and by the time the sailfish show up, there are usually also whale sharks, some species of whale, and of course, frigate birds (*Fregata magnificens*) which dive-bomb the shoal from above.

The boat captains search for sightings of these frigate birds as they are always the first telltale sign of a large group of sardines. Usually the shoal stays deep, but when they are attacked, they bunch up and rise toward the surface to seek safety in numbers.

The sailfish communicate with one another by changing color with broad stripes and flashes of silver and blue predominating. Traveling at speeds in excess of 65 knots (120kph), they are extremely efficient hunters. Working in groups of 40 individuals or more, they get into a formation by working together to attack the baitballs. There is competition out there in the ocean when sardines are around, and Minke whales, common dolphins, whale sharks, and large tuna and bonito will all join in the frenzied hunt underwater. When in attack mode, the sailfish raise their huge dorsal fins like a flag to scare the fish into swimming in a particular direction; they then sweep their long sharp beaks from side to side batting at the sardines with remarkable precision. Stunning the fish with their initial attack, they then move in for the kill and quickly devour the school.

LEFT: Atlantic sailfish in their scores hunt the packs of sardines, driving them into baitballs, where they are attacked mercilessly by these extremely efficient predators.
OPPOSITE: Whale sharks, the largest fish in the sea, are common visitors off Isla Mujeres following the plankton bloom and sardines that are driven by the might of the Gulf Stream.

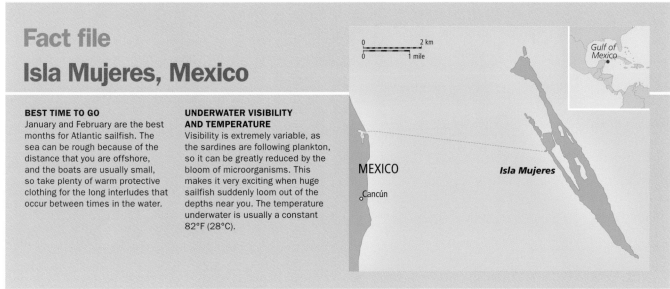

Fact file
Isla Mujeres, Mexico

BEST TIME TO GO
January and February are the best months for Atlantic sailfish. The sea can be rough because of the distance that you are offshore, and the boats are usually small, so take plenty of warm protective clothing for the long interludes that occur between times in the water.

UNDERWATER VISIBILITY AND TEMPERATURE
Visibility is extremely variable, as the sardines are following plankton, so it can be greatly reduced by the bloom of microorganisms. This makes it very exciting when huge sailfish suddenly loom out of the depths near you. The temperature underwater is usually a constant 82°F (28°C).

Gulf of Mexico

2 km

1 mile

MEXICO

Cancún

Isla Mujeres

Belize

Caribbean Sea

Belize, formerly known as British Honduras, has long been at the pinnacle of many divers' ambitions. There are several huge atolls which, with Chinchorro Reef in Mexico, are the only true coral atolls in the Caribbean region. The coast of Belize is part of a huge barrier reef that stretches from Mexico to Honduras and is known for its incredible diversity of corals, algae, fish, and invertebrates. The largest of the three atolls is Turneffe Reef which is over 35 miles (56km) long and 10 miles (16km) at its widest point. The eastern shoreline is the most exposed and in general the sea is quite rough here. Most of the diving takes place along the sheltered west coast and near the exposed corners where tidal vagaries make for some interesting drift diving and the chance to see large marine animals such as that marine giant, the whale shark (*Rinchodon typus*). Typically for this region of the Caribbean, the reef structure is "spur and groove" in configuration with small linear patches of reef running perpendicular to the shore, interspaced with narrow sandy gullies. In many instances these have overgrowth, creating interesting swimthroughs and caverns.

The southwestern zone is the most dived, but when the sea conditions permit, diving is concentrated along the east coast where you are guaranteed large numbers of jacks, trevally, permit, barracuda, and snapper. Large concentrations of Caribbean reef shark (*Carcharhinus perezi*) are common and divers should also expect to see nurse

ABOVE: Always remember to look upward, instead of concentrating solely on the coral reef in front of you, or you may miss the many turtles swimming just above you.

OPPOSITE: Curiously shaped orange rope sponges are formed by the prevailing currents around some of the more exposed corners of the coral atolls.

BELOW: Bluestriped grunt tend to keep in small groups and stay among soft corals.

sharks on most dives too. Peter's Peaks, Blue Creek, Triple Anchors, and Rendezvous Cut are all popular dives with good coral buttresses, plenty of large and colorful sponges, and masses of fish to enjoy.

Ambergris Cay is part of the barrier reef and is the closest reef to the mainland. A number of conservation initiatives have taken place here over the years due primarily to the quality of the corals and good health and diversity of the fish and invertebrate populations. Unlike the outer atolls where the diving is concentrated on the west coast, because these reefs are so much more protected by the outer atolls, the diving on Ambergris Cay is done on the east coast where large swimthroughs, corals canyons, buttress walls, and sand chutes are common. Depths here range from 50ft (15m) down into the abyss to the first submerged ledge at around 200ft (60m).

Lighthouse Reef is located 60 miles (100km) east of the mainland and some dive boats will still undertake the journey from San Pedro, leaving very early in the morning. With six large coral cays on the perimeter of the atoll, this reef is world famous for its massive **Great Blue Hole** located midway down the atoll. At over 300ft (90m) across and approximately 500ft (145m) deep, this is one of the largest blue holes on the planet. There is little coral growth

"The coast of Belize is part of a huge barrier reef that stretches from Mexico to Honduras and is known for its incredible diversity of corals, algae, fish, and invertebrates."

ABOVE: The Great Blue Hole on Lighthouse Reef is the iconic dive for all visitors to this huge Caribbean coral atoll.
OPPOSITE: Diving on some of the vertical walls is always exhilarating, as there is such a wide variety of marine life to observe, including anemones, corals, and sponges.

around the rim, but the deep interior always has large numbers of sharks. Once you get down to around 130ft (40m), you will come across the first of the huge stalactites which indicate that this collapsed cavern once stood well above sea level during the last ice age when the water level in this region was as much as 330ft (100m) lower than it is now.

Blue holes are found in shallow limestone carbonate platforms. During the time these rock formations stood above water, they were subject to the forces of erosion which eventually created great caverns of stalactites and stalagmites. These caverns gradually filled with water as the sea level rose once more. Many of the ceilings of the caverns then collapsed and so created the vertical caves known as blue holes.

Roughly circular in shape, they all have near vertical walls and are usually very deep, resulting in a water color change when viewed from above. There are pale colors in the shallows and then a rich indigo blue that is characteristic of deep blue holes.

Fact file Belize

BEST TIME TO GO
Diving is available all year round, but this region is also influenced by weather patterns in the Pacific and quite often experiences more rain than its more easterly neighbors. Hurricanes usually arrive late in the season in around October and November; the months of May through to July are usually excellent.

UNDERWATER VISIBILITY AND TEMPERATURE
Ranging from 72°F (22°C) in January to over 84°F (29°C) in August, the sea temperature does vary significantly—particularly if you dive the blue hole, as you will find a noticeable thermocline at depth where the water temperature may drop several degrees. Visibility is usually very good at over 100ft (30m). The most frequent comment that divers make about these reefs refers to the sheer scale of them. You feel very small surrounded by such a huge coral reef.

Bay Islands, Honduras

Caribbean Sea

Once part of Spain's colonial expansion into the New World, Honduras was first visited by Christopher Columbus in 1502. The country gained full independence in 1821, although that came with military rule. In 1982 Honduras elected a fully democratic government. Honduras's immediate neighbors are Guatemala, Nicaragua, and El Salvador. The Bay Islands where all the scuba diving is concentrated are found to the north and are arguably an extension of the same barrier reef that stretches from Mexico and along the coast of Belize.

The Bay Islands are comprised of Roatán, Guanaja, and Utila and are located 40 miles (64km) north of Honduras. There are several small satellites around these three main islands including the superb

Cayos Cochinos, as well as a number of raised coral seamounts that are around 60ft (18m) below the surface. The islands are coralline in structure but were forced upward through tectonic upheaval and are all now covered with lush vegetation, with precipitous walls under the surface and a very high concentration of marine life.

Utila

The smallest and flattest of the Bay Islands, Utila is renowned for the quality of its marine life, and is also quite a cheap place to stay. Very laid back but with poor internal transportation, the island is well known for its sightings of whale sharks in February and March. There are plenty of dive stores all along the main street, and they are very competitive in their bids to get your business. The whale shark sightings correspond to a plankton bloom in this southwestern region of the Caribbean and so the visibility is not as good as it can be. As Utila is mainly a low coral island, there is little freshwater runoff, and as a result the water is generally clearer and cleaner than elsewhere. In addition the large mangrove forests also filter the nutrients, as well as providing important hatcheries for reef fish, which all makes for some exceptional diving. Great Wall in particular is known for its gentle currents and superb black coral trees.

Roatán

Nearby Roatán is the largest of the islands at around 36 miles (58km) long. It is narrow with high peaks, so transport by boat is easier than by road. In fact, the best way to dive here is from a live-aboard boat, as this will give you the widest variety of dives for the least amount of effort. The barrier reefs stretch all

LEFT: Utila is renowned for the encounters that divers can have with whale sharks in February and March each year.
OPPOSITE: Jacks patrol the interface where the reef top rolls over into the depths. They are always hunting for small chromis and wrasse to consume.

the way around this island and it looks like the classic midstage of the formation of an atoll with high peaks on land, a shallow lagoon, and an outer barrier reef cut with numerous passes.

Eel Gardens dive site and **West Point** can be recommended as great dives. Eel Gardens has literally thousands of garden eels (*Heteroconger halis*) all over the shallow lagoon, bending and swaying in the slight current while picking off floating bits of plankton to eat. Flying gurnards and razor fish can be seen as well as conch shells, and stingrays with their attendant bar jacks. Many divers prefer to do Roatán's West Point at night. The dive has a gentle slope that drops from shallow water and is cut by numerous

gullies absolutely filled with marine life. Sharptail eels (*Myrichthys breviceps*) are common here as are a number of other eels which forage for sleeping fish. The colors on this reef at night are spectacular, particularly the red sponges, golden cup corals, brilliant little shrimp, and crabs and starfish.

Guanaja

The island of Guanaja to the northeast is dominated by its three large peaks. They almost form three separate islands, but are still joined together and surrounded by a barrier reef. Very reminiscent of the lagoon islands in the Pacific, these barrier reefs are cut by wide channels which were once the outlets for ancient rivers. Fresh water still permeates through the limestone in these areas and so there are only a few of the harder corals. However, at the edges of these sand chutes and ravines, the full spectrum of the Caribbean marine ecosystem can be experienced with multitudes of species vying for space.

These closely packed reefs offer superb protection for the coral growth and there are great stands of elkhorn, staghorn, boulder, and brain corals. Sponges are prevalent and all of the associated tropical marine life of the Caribbean appears to have made its home here. The West Point of Guanaja is also a favorite dive particularly as there is a separate undersea coral island, almost (but not quite) attached to the reef wall. On the outer slopes are huge black corals, whip corals, sheet corals, and an amazing variety of sponges. You may even spot your first manta ray here, as I did.

Guanaja is also well known for its superb shipwreck, the *Jado Trader*. This derelict freighter was sunk as a dive attraction back in 1987 only 1 mile (1.6km) off the southern reef, near a couple of large coral pinnacles. The conical-shaped pinnacle near the ship's bow is a perfect place to offgas as the wreck lies in 110ft (33m) of water. With only a limited time at the bottom, you can still enjoy a long dive on the reef as you swim up into shallower water. The wreck itself is covered with brilliant green and red sponges, lots of fish, and very friendly moray eels. This well-preserved ship offers a kaleidoscope of colorful marine life of every shape and form. It is a superb dive, but care must be taken amid the old rigging to avoid getting snagged.

Cayos Cochinos

Undoubtedly the marine life found around the Bay Islands is exceptional and the further you get away from the madding crowd, the better the experience becomes. Little Coco and Marjorie's Bank are ancient submarine mountains that come to 60ft (18m) below the surface. They are located midway between the Bay Islands and a small group of mountainous peaks and coral cays called Cayos Cochinos or the Hog Islands. These undersea mounts have huge schools of fusiliers, jacks, trevally, and barracuda. Although the corals are mainly low-lying, there are some massive barrel sponges, usually with lobster hiding in them. Hogfish, snapper, and grunt like to hide under the coral recesses and overall you really get the feeling of diving in the open ocean. At Cayos Cochinos you can enjoy an exceptional night dive experience.

Pelican Point Wall starts in only 10ft (3m) and drops well below the safe diving depth. You may be lucky enough to see virtually every possible species of Caribbean nudibranch here, as well as a wide variety of unusual shrimp, huge channel-clinging crabs, and almost everything else in between. The shallows have flamingo tongue shells, channel-clinging crabs, sailfin blennies, octopus, golden stingrays, and orange-ball anemones. Cayos Cochinos is a Marine Protected Area, which helps to ensure that this magical underwater environment supports the healthiest and most pristine marine life in the Bay Islands.

OPPOSITE: Yellowhead jawfish can be rather elusive, always darting back into their coral recess when you approach.

Fact file
Bay Islands, Honduras

BEST TIME TO GO
Honduras is hot and humid almost all year round. Heavily influenced by the Pacific weather patterns, regular squalls come in overland. These very green islands do experience a lot of rain, the heaviest being in the winter months. May and June are superb with light Caribbean breezes (and cool drinks!), while February is whale shark and manta season.

UNDERWATER VISIBILITY AND TEMPERATURE
The average visibility is usually around 80ft (25m) and temperatures in this latitude rarely drop below 80°F (27°C).

0	20 km
0	10 miles

Guanaja
Roatán
Jado Trader wreck
Eel Gardens West Point
The Bay Islands (Honduras)
Utila
Pelican Point *Little Coco*
Cayos Cochinos
Gulf of Mexico
La Ceiba
HONDURAS

Dutch Antilles

Caribbean Sea

Formerly known as the Netherlands Antilles, these are a large and sprawling chain of islands comprising two separate groups. To the northeast of the Caribbean are Saba, Sint Eustatius, and—shared with France—Sint Maarten/Saint Martin. In the south-central Caribbean are another group of three islands, collectively known as the ABCs; these are Aruba, Bonaire, and Curaçao. Aruba seceded in 1986 to gain autonomy, but it remained within the Kingdom of the Netherlands. The name of the Netherlands Antilles was finally discontinued in 2010 and two new constituent countries were formed: Curaçao and Sint Maarten. Bonaire, Saba, and Sint Eustatius are now classed as special municipalities of the Netherlands, yet they are still (and probably always will be) referred to as the Dutch Antilles. Dutch is the official language throughout all six islands, but American English is mainly used in the dive centers and resorts. In Curaçao and Bonaire, the language is Papiamentu which is a mix of Portuguese, Spanish, Dutch, English, and French; Curaçao is now known locally as Korsou—highly confusing, isn't it?

Curiously while these islands are relatively arid and cactus-filled, being heavily influenced by the flora and fauna of South America, all of the main towns boast classic Dutch architecture. It appears rather incongruous at first, but it really seems to fit in with the surroundings. Favored by American and Dutch divers who often return every year, many swear that this is the best diving in the Caribbean. Big business has undoubtedly "fueled" the economy, but the tourists are the ones who pay with their dive fees. Located only 40 miles (64km) north of the Venezuelan coast, the islands were originally a Spanish possession before being ceded to the Dutch in the 17th century. While the more obvious economy is based on petrochemicals and oil refining, tourism is a driving force in all of the islands.

OPPOSITE: Colorful flamingo tongue shells can be found on most sea fans, their distinctive body coloration an obvious giveaway of their presence in the water.

Aruba

The island of Aruba has developed almost independently around the amazing annual migrations of whale sharks. The local reefs are of very good quality and while a number of Caribbean islands situated within the hurricane zone have lost their elkhorn coral forests (*Acropora palmata*), here they are vibrant and intact. These huge coral colonies come very close to the surface of the water and many species of grouper, snapper, and grunt take shelter in the long shadows cast by these massive corals. Snapper City or **Pos Chiquito** has a very varied coral collection with all the usual Caribbean fish and invertebrates, including literally hundreds of flamingo tongue shells. Most of the reefs have large steep slopes which drop into the depths and you are able to gauge your dive profile according to your skill level.

The most notable diving wreck is the ***Antilla***. Scuttled during the Second World War, much of her superstructure is still high and dry and as her deepest part at the stern in only in 60ft (18m), you can enjoy seemingly endless time under water on this colorful shipwreck. Aruba is famous for offering great opportunities to swim with whale sharks, usually from December through February when the southern plankton bloom passes the islands.

Bonaire

Nearby Bonaire seems to have grabbed the lion's share of dive tourism and because of its north-to-south orientation coupled with the uninhabited satellite island, Klein Bonaire, lying to the west, the diving along the west coast is very protected. Shore diving here is promoted, although Cayman Brac can give the islands a good run for their money in the number of shore dives and quality of shore diving available. The Town Pier in particular is fabulous, but diving is limited due to its constant use by boats during the day. You really only want to dive this site at night, but when it is open it can get very busy and there is usually a cacophony of whistles and clangs from the dive masters trying to herd up their

"Favored by American and Dutch divers who often return every year, many swear that this is the best diving in the Caribbean."

"Most of the reefs have large steep slopes which drop into the depths and you are able to gauge your dive profile according to your skill level."

particular groups of divers. If you can, dive this pier independently and ignore the crowd. Most of the dive centers are very liberal and trusting and will provide stands of diving tanks ready to be uplifted at any time of the day or night, so you can dive here to your heart's content. The top wreck is the **Hilma Hooker**, an impounded drug runner that finally sank in 1984. Lying on her starboard side, she is well encrusted with marine life and sits in around 100ft (30m) near a steeply sloping coral wall to the south of the island. The reefs around Klein Bonaire can only be visited by dive boat, but sites such as Yellowman have fantastic staghorn coral (*Acropora cervicornis*) and you can usually find longlure frogfish and even sea horses here. The shallows have plenty of squid and the walls have teeming schools of creole wrasse (*Clepticus parrae*) and boga (*Haemulon vittatum*).

Curaçao

Located in the center of the group, Curaçao is aligned in a southeast to northwesterly direction with the majority of the diving located along the more sheltered western shore, principally around the capital, Willemstad. The island is very westernized and bears little, if any, resemblance to your expectation of most Caribbean islands—until you get under the water. The reefs and drop-off are superb, the edges of this rolling drop are covered in lovely sea fans, abundant anemones, and their attendant symbiotic shrimp, large stands of curiously shaped pillar coral, and several small wrecks. Although well broken up, the wrecks are still enjoyable to explore in shallow water. Curaçao's number one wreck is

ABOVE: Alien invader: the opportunistic orange cup coral
OPPOSITE: Large channel-clinging crabs venture out from their hidden crevices to feed from dusk to dawn.

undoubtedly the **Superior Producer**. En route to Venezuela in 1977 and heavily overloaded, this freighter caught the wrong wave at the entrance to the port and was quickly swamped and sank. Now resting in 105ft (32m), upright and intact, her holds are open and the entire superstructure is absolutely festooned with huge purple stove-pipe sponges (*Aplysina archeri*) and brilliant orange cup corals (*Tubastrea coccinea*). This flower coral or cup coral is an alien invader too, a bit like the lionfish. This species was first recorded in Curaçao back in 1943 attached to a ship's hull that had arrived from the Pacific. By 1971 this incredibly opportunistic coral was well established in the Virgin Islands and by 1999 it was being recorded in the Flower Gardens up in the Gulf of Mexico, attached to the support legs of an oil rig.

Fact file Dutch Antillies

BEST TIME TO GO
Outside the hurricane belt, the islands are more stable climatically and have cooling trade winds that lower the temperature and humidity. Spring and fall are great, but January and February are best for the whale sharks off Aruba.

UNDERWATER VISIBILITY AND TEMPERATURE
The visibility is usually around 80–100ft (25–30m) on most dives; some inshore reefs suffer a bit from the proximity of so much development and lack of mangroves. Average temperature is 80°F (27°C).

0   30 km
0   20 miles

Caribbean Sea

Antilla wreck
Aruba (Netherlands)
Oranjestad
Pos Chiquito

Netherlands Antilles (Netherlands)
Bonaire
Curacao
Willemstad
Klein Bonaire
Hilma Hooker Kralendijk
Superior Producer wreck
wreck

VENEZUELA

Tobago

Caribbean Sea

The Democratic Republic of Trinidad and Tobago has a combined population of approximately 1,305,000. The islands are situated safely outside the hurricane belt in the southeastern corner of the Windward Islands. They lie on the continental shelf of South America with just over 12 miles (20km) separating them. Geographically they are generally considered to be located entirely in South America.

Their economy is largely based around petroleum, chemicals, tourism, and food processing. Oil was first discovered off the west coast of Trinidad in 1866, but production did not begin until 1908. Oil output proved to be abundant, and it was necessary to bring in an Indian and Asian workforce to help harvest this natural bounty. This has resulted in a diverse racial mix. While English is generally spoken, French, Hindi, and Spanish are also used, as well as a local French patois. The populations of both islands are religious and a wide variety of religions are practiced.

While Trinidad and Tobago are usually mentioned together, they are quite dissimilar. Tobago is more dependent on the tourism industry. It is a favorite dive destination and so the diving industry has burgeoned with many local people working in the sport, which forms a large part of the island's economy. Trinidad is less orientated toward diving although it can offer some superb and very underrated diving around the northwestern point in an area known as the Chaguaramas Peninsula. This is a small strand of tiny islands and sheltered bays that stretch out toward Venezuela.

Music is the pulse of life and these islands have an amazing musical history and can claim to be the origin of the steel drum. The advent of the steel band, calypso, and soca music in the Caribbean means Carnival Time and no one does it better than Tobago. It is well worth experiencing this haunting ethnic mix of Asian, Indian, African, and British sounds, blending together in a peaceful racial harmony as you listen to some of the most soulful music ever played.

Tobago occupies a land area of about 120sq miles (310km^2) and is 25 miles (40km) long and 7.5 miles (12km) at its widest point. Tobago has encouraged eco-development, and some resorts on this small island are considerably more eco-friendly than some of its larger neighbors. Tobago has one of the oldest protected rainforests in the world. This forested area supports great biodiversity including many species of birds, mammals, frogs, (nonpoisonous) snakes, butterflies, and other invertebrates. It is one of the most approachable areas of rainforest, since it is relatively small and there are government-appointed guides who provide an authoritative guiding service through the forest at a reasonable cost. The guides are knowledgeable about the plants and the animals, and can call down rare and exotic birds from the canopy by imitating their calls. Tobago also has nesting beaches for the leatherback turtle, and the females come to shore between April and July to lay their eggs in the sand.

There is a peaceful calm to the islands, but in the sea amazing currents surge between them from the Atlantic and up from the Orinoco Delta. Tobago's underwater scenery is just as impressive with caves, caverns, natural arches, and offshore seamounts. The waters, fed by the Guiana Current, are nutrient-rich and support an abundance of marine life. The islands' proximity to the Atlantic coupled with the protected shorelines of the Caribbean result in an outstanding combination of both warm and colder water species. Large numbers of pelagics can be seen here and this is one of the world's permanent locations for manta rays and endemic species that are not found anywhere else.

Speyside

Tobago is aligned in a southwest to northeast direction. In the northeast of the island lies the region known as Speyside. Unlike other islands in

OPPOSITE: Manta rays are encountered off Speyside in Tobago all year round due to the nutrient-rich waters from the Guiana Current that push northward through the islands.

"... this is one of the world's permanent locations for manta rays and endemic species that are not found anywhere else."

the Windward Island chain, which have established their diving predominantly on the western Caribbean-influenced coast, most of the diving in Tobago is concentrated in a small area which is protected from the might of the Atlantic swells by Little Tobago Island and Goat Island. These islands are well known not only for their lush fringing reefs, but also for the strength of the currents that sweep up around the corner and through the inner passage between the outer islands and mainland Tobago. The Speyside diving region is within the bay to the west and south of Little Tobago Island and includes the reefs around Goat Island located closer to shore. With regular sightings of giant manta rays, large schools of tarpon, and even sharks, Speyside has some of the best diving in Tobago.

The majority of the dives are drift dives and so they are largely dependent on the strength of the large oceanic surge. The largest brain corals (*Colpophyllia natans*) ever recorded in the northern hemisphere are found here. Just south of Little Tobago on a dive site called **Kelleston Drain** lies the largest recorded brain coral in the world, measuring 10ft by 16ft (3m x 4.75m). The unbelievable shoals of tiny fish and the likelihood of seeing manta rays are a magnet that draws regular divers back time after time. Black Jack Hole, Book Ends, Angel Reef, and the Washing Machine are also well worth diving. Some are

more challenging than others, but all yield a higher than average population of marine life.

At the north of the island is a natural arch called **London Bridge** and while the surge may prove too strong to negotiate it, the walls and seabed are covered in sea fans, brilliant sponges, and rare anemones with their attendant symbiotic shrimp. The Saint Giles Islands are really not much more than a group of offshore rocks but their oceanic exposure results in good sightings of whale sharks and massive schools of trevally and jacks.

To the south of the island is a shallow reef platform that stretches out toward Trinidad. If you wish to experience the rush of a 5-knot (9-kph) current in the open ocean, then strap on your wings as you will "fly" over the limestone ridges topped with curiously shaped sponges and corals bent over by the incessant tidal movement. Nurse sharks, turtles, and numerous angelfish are all found here on the dive known as **Diver's Dream**.

OPPOSITE: The largest brain corals in the northern hemisphere are found in Tobago's Speyside area.
BELOW: Balloonfish are often found in pairs. They have light-sensitive eyes, and are regularly found foraging for food on most night dives.

"The largest brain corals ever recorded in the northern hemisphere are found here."

Fact file Tobago

BEST TIME TO GO
The humidity is often as high as 80%, but temperatures are more stable and cooled by the constant Atlantic trade winds. The dry season is January to May; April to June is best for sightings of leatherback turtles; September to November is best for the reefs. You can see mantas almost any time of the year, but April and May are the prime months.

UNDERWATER VISIBILITY AND TEMPERATURE
Visibility is around 80ft (25m) although this can be greatly reduced during the spring plankton bloom. However, this is when you also have a better chance of seeing the big marine creatures. Water temperature averages 78°F (26°C), but can drop sharply in the winter to around 68°F (20°C).

Caribbean Sea

0   5 km
0   3 miles

Saint Giles Islands
London Bridge
Goat Island
Little Tobago
Speyside
Kelleston Drain

Tobago

Scarborough

Diver's Dream

St. Lucia

Caribbean Sea

St. Lucia is the second largest of the Windward Islands located 110 miles (175km) northwest of Barbados and almost equidistant between Martinique in the north and St. Vincent to the south. It was discovered by explorer Christopher Columbus on December 13, 1502—the Feast of St. Lucy— and so he named it Santa Lucia. Originally owned by the French, who first settled the island in 1650, it became a British dependency in 1814. St. Lucia gained full independence in 1979 and is a member of the British Commonwealth.

The island is mountainous and very pretty, supporting huge banana plantations. The volcanic peaks are topped by Mt. Gimie, the highest mountain at 3,117ft (950m). The island is probably better known for the two peaks to the south of the town of Soufrière that were created when Mt. Soufrière exploded—the **Pitons**. They are spectacular, dominating the landscape both above and underwater. Incidentally the local beer is also called Piton!

Situated on the southeast coast of St. Lucia, just north of the region's main town Soufrière, **Anse Chastanet** is a small designated marine park that boasts so much marine life you could spend years discovering and describing the different species. If you are a photographer, you may rate dive sites according to the richness of the photographs that they are likely to yield, rather than whether they are exciting drift dives, technical deep dives onto wrecks or reefs, or even particularly spectacular in terms of archways, tunnels, or cliffs. In this respect, the marine park in front of the Anse Chastanet resort is one of the highest yielding dive sites for marine life species in the entire Caribbean.

Accompanied by very experienced dive guides, you will discover that this marine nature reserve has a shallow platform with sandy gullies between low coral spurs and a near vertical wall in some places that drops to well below the safe diving depth. And it is all located just a few yards from the shore. The high biodiversity is often linked to the island's volcanic interior, with its hot water vents and sulfurous conditions. On the one hand this gives the water a greenish tinge, but on the other it means it is able to sustain exotic creatures which are found in more remote parts of the Caribbean. For this and many other reasons, Anse Chastanet is one of the top shore reef sites to dive at night in the Caribbean.

As you enter the water in front of the Scuba St. Lucia dive store, most divers tend to go left along the edge of the wall and sand slope and work in among the coral heads. This is a dive that you can do at almost any depth that takes your fancy, particularly if you have already enjoyed some diving on the same day. There are electric rays, golden rays, and some rather weird invertebrates which are generally not found in these regions. I have even photographed a species of shrimp which is thought to be new to science. Paul Humann and Ned DeLoach who produced the *Reef* set of books about Caribbean marine life species photographed more odd creatures here than anywhere else in the Caribbean.

ABOVE: Spotted moray eels are commonly seen on most dives around St. Lucia. They are unafraid of divers.
OPPOSITE: Long-spined sea urchins, deepwater gorgonian sea fans, colorful crinoids, and sponges are likely to be encountered on every dive.

ABOVE: Delicate tube worms are light- and pressure-sensitive and immediately hide should you get too close and disturb their quest for microscopic plankton.

OPPOSITE: Frogfish are only spotted rarely in the Caribbean due to their superb camouflage. This red frogfish is mimicking the appearance of the red sponge above it.

Fact file St. Lucia

BEST TIME TO GO
The hurricane season is from June through to November. April and May are excellent with lots of sun, calm, clear water, and the best conditions overall.

UNDERWATER VISIBILITY AND TEMPERATURE
Visibility is often reduced due to the volcanic nature of the islands and averages around 50ft (15m). Temperature is cooler in the winter and influenced by the Atlantic Ocean and will drop below 72°F (22°C).

TRAVEL ADVICE
Once a British colony, the electric power is 220 volts using British-style three-pin square plugs. American-style 110-volt adapters are available from the hotels, or alternatively use the two-pin shaver socket.

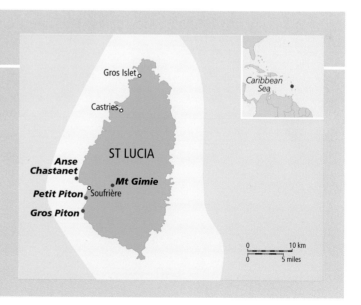

Continuing in a circuitous loop of the dive site and staying in under 40ft (12m) of water, you can follow the sandy gullies through the coral heads until you reach the sand slope directly in front of the shore, which plummets into the depths to your left. With the vertical reef wall also dropping off to your left and the sand slope stretching up into the shallows, the reflected lights from the Anse Chastanet resort are visible on the surface of the water. However, this is not the end of your dive. Interspaced in the sand slope are small patches of coral which are a veritable oasis of life. Here you will find the very rare golden coral shrimp (*Stenopus scutellatus*) which is similar to the very common banded coral shrimp (*Stenopus hispidus*), although the two are deadly enemies. The sandy patches yield burrowing starfish, rare delicate tube anemones, heart urchins, peacock flounders, and many species of nudibranch and sea hare. Close to the shore you may see resident electric rays and a couple of species of mantis shrimp that are new to science. This is perhaps the best night dive from any shore on any reef in the Caribbean. Yes, there are other superb sites but they are all difficult to get to and not at all like this shallow shore dive at Anse Chastanet in St. Lucia. This should not be missed—at any time of day.

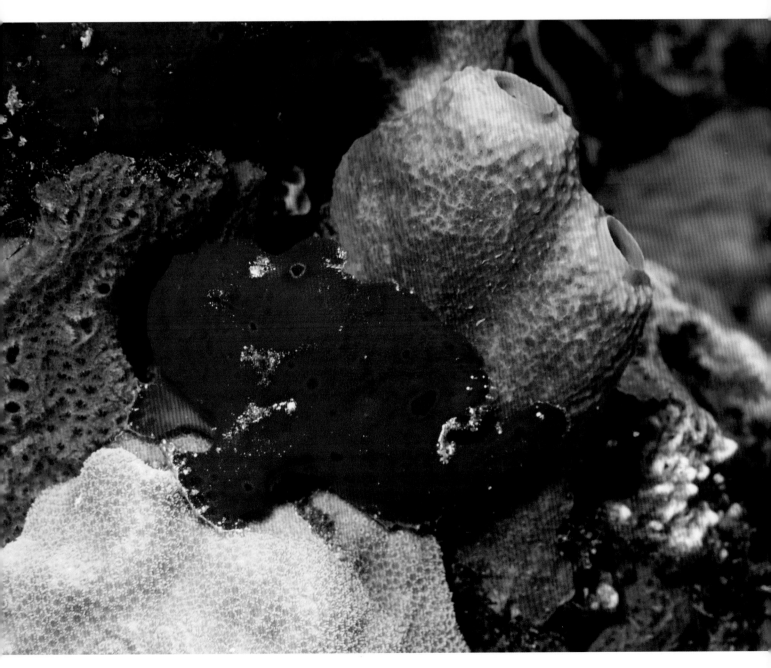

Dominica

Caribbean Sea

Dominica is relatively young by geological standards and indeed the entire chain of islands here reveal evidence of geothermal activity, such as hot springs, boiling lakes, molten pitch or tar, underwater vents, and sulfurous gas outflow. Like nearby Montserrat, the top of the island blew off in 1995 when its "dormant" volcano erupted, spewing lava and ash all over the island. Dominica's underwater vents are famous for their sulfur bubbles and one dive site is even called "Champagne." (Strangely, even though you are wearing a mask underwater, you can still "smell" the sulfur.)

Nicknamed the Nature Isle of the Caribbean, the island was named by Columbus after the day of the week on which it was first sighted (a Sunday—*Domenica* in Italian). The French subsequently gained possession of the island but ceded it to Britain in 1763. Dominica gained full independence in 1978 and is a member of the British Commonwealth.

Dominica is flanked by the French colonies of Guadeloupe to the north and Martinique to the south. Many of the locals speak a type of French, Carib, and West African creole known as Kwéyòl.

The Kalinago, who are descended from the original Carib Indians, still live by traditional fishing and farming methods. They are distinctive in appearance, resembling South American Amazon tribespeople although much shorter in stature. The Kalinago name for the island is Wai'tukubuli.

Dominica is extremely mountainous: two of the peaks are over 4,500ft (1,300m). The topography is stunning with fantastic rainforest fauna and flora all found amidst cloud-topped peaks, dramatic gorges, caverns, waterfalls, and hidden lakes. It is now recognized as a World Heritage Site. The underwater reefs also resemble more tropical dive sites due to the rarity of curious fish species, thousands of colorful crinoids, black coral forests, and superb vibrant sponges.

Roseau to Portsmouth

Most of the diving is done on the western, sheltered, Caribbean side of the island. The mountainous terrain on land descends just as far into the depths and a number of dive sites appear like bottomless pits fringed with coral. The Caribbean coastline of Dominca is favored by a large number of cetaceans including Bryde's whale, pilot whales, pygmy sperm whales, and sperm whales, spinner dolphins, bottlenose dolphins, pantropical dolphins, Fraser's dolphins, and spotted dolphins. Orca are found here and although they have the "whale" tag, they are also part of the dolphin superfamily that includes the false killer whale (*Pseudorca crassidens*).

A special license from the Ministry of Agriculture and Fisheries is required to enter the water with the cetaceans and to assist in the research of the migration patterns of the various cetacean species.

LEFT: Giant barrel sponges are common on Dominica, particularly around the area known as Danglebens.
OPPOSITE: These false killer whales have corralled a juvenile common dolphin, which is likely to be considered prey by these cooperative hunters.

Some very long and uncomfortable hours are usually spent well offshore, but with the research vessel's underwater hydrophone, scientists can locate a number of pods of sperm whales. Different species of dolphin often frolic in the boat's bow-spray and an encounter with these magnificent beasts is always a magical experience.

The first sperm whale that I saw was a juvenile calf which "spy-hopped" as it came by the boat. His regular fin strokes far outmatched our pace and all too soon he was gone. Others soon showed up, but they would "sound" before we could get near them.

After a two-day lull with no activity, the distinctive dark bulbous heads of some false killer whales were spotted. Around 12 of this group had approached our boat is stealth mode (keeping completely quiet underwater) until we spotted them breaching. On entering the water, the group eyed us with their sly grins and big toothy smiles, but it was a lonely common dolphin that had caught their eye. This beast was soon herded into the middle of the pack and it was obvious that the creature was not going to be allowed to escape. The "killers" kept it hemmed in and ushered it away from our group to an unknown fate.

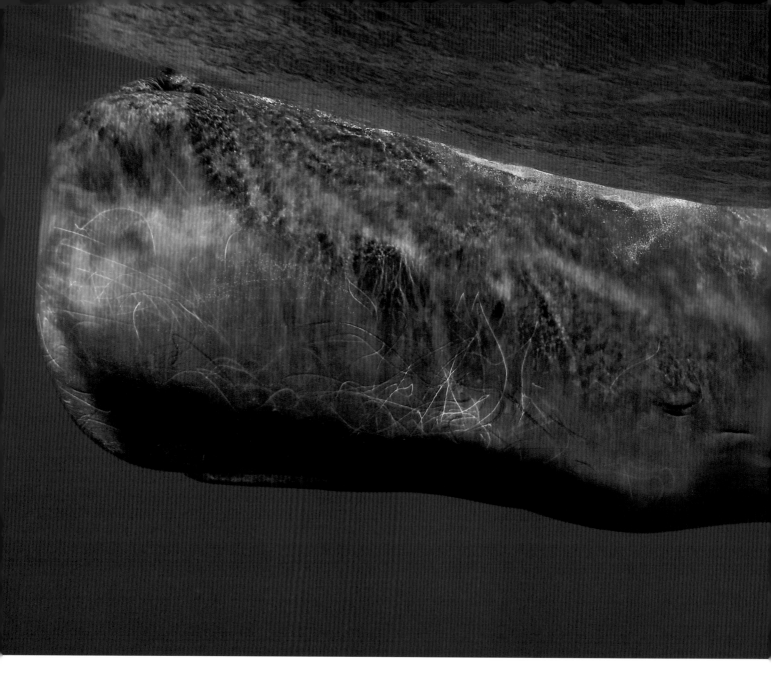

Danglebens

Further away to the south by dive boat is the caldera of an extinct volcano called Danglebens. Close to shore, part of the rim rises up in a rocky spur, while other areas are lower and form a series of seamounts which disappear into the depths where the outer edge has completely disappeared.

The area is very rich in marine life, perhaps as a result of the volcanic activity, the slightly warmer water, and sulfurous bubbles. Many varieties of sponge and colorful crinoids can be seen, and the entire Danglebens area is more like a Pacific reef with crustaceans and fish that are rarely seen anywhere else in the Caribbean. The coral pinnacles come to within 40ft (12m) of the surface and are connected by a coral "saddle" before dropping into the depths. You may encounter dozens of spotted moray eels

(*Gymnothorax moringa*) and, possibly, a very curious mix of subspecies of hamlet (*Hypoplectrus* spp.). There are so many interbreeding species here that scientists are looking at several new classifications of the species. A fascinating crustacean here is the red banded lobster (*Justitia longimanus*), which is extremely rare elsewhere in the Caribbean. Considered only nocturnal in habit, individuals have occasionally been seen during afternoon dives, which is a puzzling departure from their usual behavior. The usual show of creole wrasse, yellowhead wrasse, and blue and green chromis are everywhere in the water column, as are yellowtail snapper, bar jacks, and plentiful barracuda.

The nearby reef at night is likely to yield electric rays, curious unidentified shrimp, and some fish that are suffering from parasitic isopods. These odd

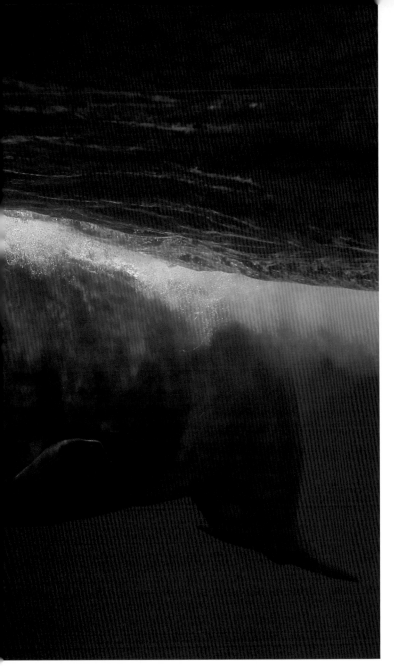

crustaceans attach themselves around the heads of several small grouper, squirrelfish, and angelfish and live directly off the blood and tissue of their host. You may also see many hermit crabs, bubble-tipped anemones, starfish, sea spiders, basket stars, and all manner of weird and wonderful creatures not usually seen during the day.

Slightly further north, most of the small B&Bs and resorts lie south of the capital Roseau and all have direct access onto the rocky shore. Clearly volcanic in origin, the shoreline is difficult to scramble over, but once in the water the seabed slopes away steeply. There are large groups of garden eels (*Heteroconger halis*). Small coral heads are lush and act like mini-oases with all manner of creatures creating a working biosphere. Prey and predators often line up together to be cleaned of parasites by cleaner shrimp at the various cleaning stations which are to be found all along the reef.

Dominica is full of surprises in its marine biodiversity, from the very largest ocean-traveling mammal to the tiniest parasitic creature. The colors and variety of life both above and below the waves make this one of the most breathtaking places to dive in the Caribbean.

LEFT: Sperm whales are one of the largest cetaceans on the planet and each year several groups migrate to the clear abundant waters off Dominica's west coast to hunt squid and to give birth to their young.

Fact file **Dominica**

BEST TIME TO GO
Dominica has a typically subtropical climate with rain recorded every month, but the temperature averages out at around 77°F (25°C). Dolphins and whales are always seen, but January to March are the best months for sperm whales.

UNDERWATER VISIBILITY AND TEMPERATURE
Visibility is usually around 80ft (25m) inshore, but greatly exceeds that once you get offshore after the whales. The water temperature averages around 80°F (27°C), but does drop in the winter months. It is best to wear a full suit particularly when offshore in a small boat.

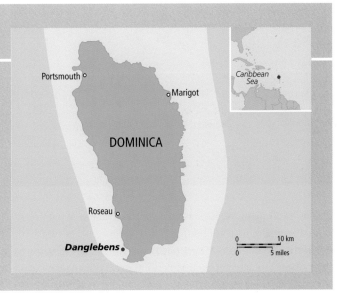

British Virgin Islands

Caribbean Sea

The remains of a huge subterranean mountain plateau that blew up millennia ago, the islands were visited by Columbus during his second exploration of the West Indies in 1493. There were so many islands visible here that he collectively named them *"Los Once Mil Virgines"* after St. Ursula and her 11,000 virgin followers. The islands are located 60 miles (95km) east of Puerto Rico and 1,100 miles (1,800 km) southeast of Miami. Although they were "discovered" by Columbus, the first visitors to the islands had been Ciboney, Arawak, and Carib Indians and a number of their artefacts have been found on the offshore islands. They were followed by British adventurers, Dutch and Spanish explorers, plantation owners, Quakers, and marauding pirates, including Blackbeard, possibly the most infamous of all. He is reputed to have punished 15 mutiny-minded men by

ABOVE: Red mullet are always seen in the evening and on night dives feeding on the seabed.

OPPOSITE: Caribbean reef octopuses are always out foraging at night. They change color sporadically from a brilliant pale blue to dazzling shades of orange and red.

putting them ashore on the island of Dead Chest, a small scrubby landmass situated between Salt Island and Peter Island to the south of Road Town.

Primarily known for their excellent cruising and safe anchorages in a multitude of secluded bays and inlets, the Virgin Islands are rapidly becoming one of the most popular diving destinations in the Caribbean. The island group is split into two distinct and entirely separate areas. To the north are the British Virgin Islands, which are a British Crown Colony and to the south lie the United States Virgin Islands, an unincorporated territory of the USA. Formerly known as the Danish West Indies they are situated a few miles southeast of Tortola, but are worlds apart culturally. Approximately 40 miles (64km) south across The Narrows lies the largest of the Virgin Islands, St. Croix. It is frequently called the "American Paradise," which is fine for Americans who enjoy a tropical home from home, but can be somewhat daunting for divers when you are faced with hordes of cruise ship passengers being disgorged into the towns.

The British Virgin Islands consist of Tortola, Virgin Gorda, Jost Van Dyke, and Anegada which lies 25 miles (40km) to the northeast of Tortola. Anegada has a massive barrier reef that stretches away to the east and southeast of this very low-lying scrubby island. The reef is renowned for being treacherous and its huge stands of elkhorn coral that sit just below the surface have ripped the hulls out of many a vessel. More shipwrecks are found here than anywhere else in the Caribbean. Treasure ships from the Spanish fleet, slave ships, livestock transporters, all have met their doom on these reefs.

If you ever get the chance to dive these reefs on a live-aboard dive boat, the rewards are spectacular, especially in an area called **Horseshoe Reef**, where the wreck of the ***Rocus*** can be found. Carrying a cargo of animal bones from Trinidad to Baltimore, she ran aground in 1929 and is now totally destroyed and covered with all manner of corals. The reef's geographical position probably accounts for the diversity of marine life found around these islands.

Fact file
British Virgin Islands

BEST TIME TO GO

Although the islands are classed as having a subtropical climate, this is tempered by the cool breezes from the Atlantic, but they do little to reduce the humidity which can get as high as the 90% here. Hurricane season tends to be late in around October and November with increased rainfall and wind. June through September can be very hot at over 104°F (40°C), but the sea can be like glass and perfect for diving.

UNDERWATER VISIBILITY AND TEMPERATURE

There is usually a spring plankton bloom in March and April which can reduce the visibility and produce a greenish cast to the water. The sea is cooler in the winter but will rise to around 80°F (27°C) during the summer months.

0   10 km
0   5 miles

Anegada
Rocus wreck
Horseshoe Reef

Virgin Islands (UK)
Chikuzen wreck
Necker Island
Oil Nut Bay
Virgin Gorda

Tortola
Road Town
Sir Francis Drake Channel

RMS Rhone
Salt Island

Gulf of Mexico

Another notable wreck in the vicinity is the **Chikuzen**, which sank between Anegada and Great Camanoe in 1981. A former Japanese refrigerated transport that had been mothballed in St. Maarten, she was due to be sunk but ended up being swept away in a storm and arrived in the BVIs. Now lying on her port side in around 80ft (25m) with her hatches open, she is a natural oasis for fish which always congregate around the wreck.

BELOW: Exploring the small caverns and swimthroughs is always rewarding as the walls are covered with colorful encrusting marine life—but do remember a flashlight.

Virgin Gorda and Necker Island

Clustered around the Sir Francis Drake Channel are a further 50 islands and cays. Named after the English explorer who sailed through the islands in 1585 en route to conquering Hispaniola, the channel is the connecting waterway between the Atlantic Ocean and the Caribbean Sea. Virgin Gorda has huge granite boulders on some of the beaches that are very reminiscent of Praslin and La Digue in the Seychelles. Although not known as widely for its diving, the sport takes place around her outer satellites, such as the reef at Oil Nut Bay which stretches between Sir Richard Branson's Necker Island and Virgin Gorda. The Seal Dogs and various other Dog Rocks all have

ABOVE: Blackbar soldierfish are very common around the wreck of the RMS *Rhone*, hiding amid its superstructure.

a number of good shallow dives offering a great selection of Caribbean marine life.

All of the islands to the east of the channel have great dive sites. While many of the shallow reefs are smothered in fire coral, everyone comes here to experience one of the top wrecks to be found underwater in the Caribbean: the **RMS *Rhone***.

This mail steamer had been sheltering outside Great Harbour on Peter Island in October 1867. A hurricane of simply massive proportions came out of the most unlikely of directions—the northwest—causing the ship to drag her anchors. A nearby ship, the *Conway*, tried to make a run for safety but the storm removed her funnel and masts and she ended up on the shores of Tortola. Captain Wooley in charge of the *Rhone* tried to weigh anchor, but the chain snapped and she lost both the anchor and chain. The wind shifted direction as the eye of the hurricane passed over them and the *Rhone* was dashed against the shore of nearby Salt Island. Tragically, 17 passengers and 108 crew lost their lives that night. Some survivors clung onto the ship's mast that was

still above water for more than 17 hours before they were rescued. There is a memorial grave on Salt Island for those who lost their lives.

There are two main sections of the wreckage. One shallow and the other deep. Although negotiable on a single dive, it is obviously easier to start off deep on the foremost section of the ship with her long bowsprit lying over on her starboard side. Continuing into shallow water past large sections of ribs and boilers and other coral-covered mechanical parts, you finally arrive at her propshaft, propeller, and stern. This is a superb wreck and one of the top dives in the Caribbean, particularly at night as the colors of the encrusting corals and sponges are simply amazing. Masses of squirrelfish, parrotfish, snapper, grunt, and wrasse swim all around, as well as a multitude of the smaller creatures such as shrimp, flamingo tongue shells, and nudibranchs.

Florida, USA

Gulf of Mexico/Atlantic Ocean

Probably more Americans dive in Florida than at any other place on the planet. When you consider the size of this ancient fishhook-shaped peninsula that traverses the Gulf Stream, the ease of the transport system to get you down to the Sunshine State, the relatively cheap accommodation, and the incredible diversity of coral reefs, historic and modern shipwrecks, freshwater caves and caverns, encounters with large wild animals, coupled with a laid-back style of life, then you can see the attraction. In fact American divers can experience almost the full range of Caribbean-style diving without leaving their own country.

Some of the largest artificial reefs in the world have been sunk off the east and west coasts and Florida Keys. The tourism board which promotes the area is also incredibly switched on and has a huge annual budget for promotion and advertising. Whatever it takes to get divers down there, they will do it and that includes sinking truly spectacular artificial reefs. Off Pensacola in the Panhandle area is the largest ship deliberately sunk as a diver attraction: in 2006 the **USS Oriskany** was scuttled in over 200ft (60m) of water while the shallowest part of the ship is at 80ft (24m). This massive aircraft carrier lay so well offshore, in a clean sandy area, that inevitably she soon developed a crusty coat of algae, sponges, small corals, and plenty of fish and invertebrates. Simply massive in scale at 911ft (277m) in length, this wreck is best suited to technical divers, but most sport divers are able to have a great dive to about 100ft (30m) as there is just so much to see.

Moving south down the west coast are found a series of crystal-clear pools at a constant 72°F (22°C) temperature. A remnant of the last ice age when this region was well above sea level, there are huge interconnecting caverns filled with stalagmites and stalactites, very similar to the blue holes of the Bahamas and the cenoté of the Yucatán in Mexico. **Ginnie Springs** is a very popular diving attraction and with its constant temperature, it is dived throughout the winter months.

The rivers, of course, are another attraction and the world-famous **Crystal River** is home to an overwintering population of sea cows or manatees. This mighty spring pumps out 650 million gallons (2,460 million liters) of clear warm water every day, and the manatees congregate around a number of favored outlets to bask in the warm water, and eat the fast-growing grass and weed which is their staple diet. The center of these springs is called "the main boil" and the cows give birth in these locations around the end of November.

Trichechus manatus latirostris, the Florida manatee or sea cow, is found on coastal and inland waterways from Brazil to Virginia in the United States. The most common location is on the northwest coast of Florida. These are the largest vegetarian creatures in the sea, weighing more than 3,000lb (1,360kg) and growing to a length of 13ft (4m). They are often mistakenly seen as a cross between a seal and a whale, but in fact they are relatives of the elephant.

Most of the time, manatees are fairly solitary creatures, but they do retain family groupings. It is only during the winter that they congregate in large herds. The manatee population was thought to be fairly stable in Florida waters, but an average of 200 deaths occur each year due to natural causes, red tide (an algae bloom), and boating accidents. Unfortunately, speed limits for boats are unrestricted between March and November each year, and most of the animals now bear telltale propeller scars across their backs.

Whether you agree with the practice of introducing large numbers of tourists alongside the manatee families or not, one thing is certain: the beasts do not appear to mind the intrusion and the local economy enjoys a huge hike upward during the winter months.

OPPOSITE: Manatees by nature are curious and friendly, but their very lifestyle is at threat due to the constant pressures of an urbanized environment and increasing tourism.

"They are often mistakenly seen as a cross between a seal and a whale, but in fact they are relatives of the elephant."

Florida Keys

Over on the east coast, from Jacksonville down through Daytona, Fort Lauderdale, and Miami, are a large number of offshore reefs and wrecks, all of which get their fair share of visitors. But most divers head down to the Florida Keys. Here there are superb offshore reefs, an abundance of fish and invertebrate species, plenty of historic wrecks—many dating back to the time of Spanish treasure ships—and now a plethora of artificial reefs which appear to be on most divers' list of must-do's! The largest of these is the *General Hoyt S. Vandenberg*. Once used as a movie prop for a Hollywood epic, she was deliberately sunk in 2010. A former troopship and missile-tracking vessel, she is over 522ft (159m) long and sits upright on the seabed. She is instantly recognizable by her two large 40ft (12m) diameter radar dishes, massive deck structures, and easily negotiable interior. Visibility and current can often be a challenge this far out into the Gulf Stream, but the rewards are well worth it, with regular sightings of large pelagic fish including amberjack and barracuda. The Dry Tortugas to the south, where the amazing Fort Jefferson is located, have always been a favorite with divers and snorkelers, but all of this diving involves fairly lengthy boat rides.

Moving up the Keys in that wide sweep of mangrove swamps, sand cays, and incredible bridges are the delightful reefs around **Marathon**, which has more fish species recorded than anywhere else in Florida. Again these reefs lie offshore, but bull sharks are regularly seen in the channels under the bridges. In **Islamorada** a few dive centers will run you out by Alligator Key near where the wreck of the *Eagle* is located. Lying on her starboard side the wreck is more or less intact, but has a large open section in front of the main wheelhouse area where the ship has broken apart. Every inch of the surface of this 1985 wreck is covered with marine life many layers deep with the most brilliant yellow cup corals vying for space with purple soft corals, brilliant red sponges, gorgeous queen angelfish, hamlets, chromis, many species of wrasse, and parrotfish. Deliberately sunk by the Florida Keys Artificial Reef Association, this is the perfect wreck on which to do two dives back-to-back to explore the entire length of the superstructure.

OPPOSITE: Lying off Key West, the superstructure of the *General Hoyt S. Vandenberg* is awesome and the ever-present American flag is quite a backdrop to this massive shipwreck.

ABOVE: The imposing statue—Christ of the Abyss—has been underwater for over 40 years and is visited daily by hundreds of divers and snorkelers.

Fact file Florida, USA

BEST TIME TO GO
Diving is available all year round. The manatees are most accessible from January to March. Offshore storms along the east coast of Florida are always a problem, but for the most part all of the reefs and wrecks are manageable. Hurricane season is traditionally June through to November, but the summer months also yield the best visibility.

UNDERWATER VISIBILITY AND TEMPERATURE
Underwater visibility is generally around 60–100ft (18–30m) in the freshwater springs. The inshore reefs along the Keys average around 50ft (15m) with greater visibility the further you travel offshore. The freshwater temperature is a constant 72°F (22°C). The sea temperature rarely drops below this in the winter months and increases by 10°F (5.5°C) on average, depending on the strength of the Gulf Stream.

Pensacola   USA   Jacksonville

USS Oriskany wreck   *Ginnie Springs*   Daytona Beach

Crystal River

St Petersburg   Florida

0   200 km
0   100 miles

Fort Lauderdale

Islamorada   *Key Largo*   Miami

General Hoyt S. Vandenberg wreck   *Molasses Reef*

Florida Keys   *Eagle wreck*

Dry Tortugas   *Marathon*

Gulf of Mexico

Key Largo

The island of Key Largo in the north is considered the epicenter for the majority of divers and in fact this long thin island attracts customers traveling both south and north, with most people diving on the wrecks and the reefs. As a result there are more dive centers here than on any other island in the Keys. The Pennekamp State National Marine Park is the first marine preserve in the United States and is celebrated by a wonderful statue known as the Christ of the Abyss. It was created originally by Italian sculptor Guido Galletti for a European industrialist called Edidi Cressi. He presented a bronze cast of it to the Underwater Society of America, and it has been submerged for over 40 years and has been visited by thousands of divers and snorkelers. This region often experiences poor visibility, but nothing detracts from the impressive statue or the condition of the reefs themselves that are found nearby.

Nearby **Molasses Reef** to the north is well known for its excellent visibility underwater. It is very shallow and gets lots of sunlight to brighten it up even on the dullest day. The well-scattered wreckage of the *City of Washington* in an area known as The Elbow is superb in only 20ft (6m) of water. Better known for her role in rescuing the survivors of the American battleship USS *Maine* when she blew up in mysterious circumstances in Havana harbor, Cuba in 1898, the *Washington* sank during a storm in 1917 and is now very much a part of this great coral reef. Friendly turtles, green moray eels, and masses of snapper and grunt are synonymous with this shallow reef.

Further offshore lie three other ships sunk as part of the artificial reef program: the *Bibb*, the *Duane*, and the *Spiegel Grove*. Unlike the many ships that have foundered naturally (or accidentally), these ships were sunk specifically as dive attractions and are a natural magnet for all kinds of sea life. Amazingly,

ABOVE: A green moray eel has made the bows of the ship its home as it offers security and space to maneuver safely.
OPPOSITE: The wreck of the *Duane* is magnificent and every part of her superstructure is completely encrusted with golden cup corals and colorful clams. Schools of fish and turtles are seen on every dive.

when the *Spiegel Grove* was first sunk, she ended up on her port side. However, a few years and a few hurricanes later, she was put back on an even keel, a remarkable feat. The **Benwood**, which lies between them, was a casualty of a German submarine attack during the Second World War and was subsequently rammed accidentally by a "friendly" ship. Later, several bombs exploded amidships and sent her to the bottom. Well broken up now, her remains are scattered over a large area in around 40ft (12m) of water and are encrusted in coral and sponge growth and surrounded by fish.

The *Duane* and the *Bibb* were former US Coastguard cutters and they were sunk deliberately on November 27, 1987 in relatively deep water over 100ft (30m), so that they would not pose a problem for navigation. Consequently these dives are regarded as deep wreck dives and with available time underwater always a problem at depth, it means that you have to return several times to fully appreciate them. The current, as always, can be a problem when you are so far out in the Gulf Stream, but the rewards are utterly astounding. These wrecks to the east of the "islands in the stream" should be on everyone's diving list. In a quick visit, and with only limited time at depth, it is difficult to gain a true perspective of this dive site. The colors, often hidden during the daylight hours, are revealed in their full glory after dusk.

Bahamas

Eastern Caribbean Sea

The islands of the Bahamas, first discovered by Christopher Columbus in 1492, are situated only 30 minutes flying time due east and south of Florida in the eastern Caribbean. Geologically, the Bahamas were once the tips of a huge plateau which stood more than 300ft (90m) above sea level during the last Ice Age. As the ice melted, the waters rose, transforming the plateau into a vast submerged bank with waters just a few feet deep. Most visitors to the 3,000 or more islands and cays get their first glimpse of them from the air and these shallow colorful waters have become a tourist magnet.

The shallow banks are a prolific nursery for all manner of fish and invertebrate life. The highest peaks of those ancient mountains remained above sea level and are now the islands favored by many discerning tourists. The larger islands of New Providence, Andros, and Grand Bahama are also home to some of the most varied and spectacular scuba diving in the Caribbean.

This is world-class diving with excellent visibility, warm waters, wrecks, caverns, blue holes, a superabundance of fish, stingrays, dolphins, sharks, and whales. Different areas of the Caribbean are famous for particular diving attractions, such as the stingrays on Grand Cayman Island, the walls and drift diving of Cozumel, and the wrecks in Bermuda. However, the Bahamas have all of these in profusion and in several locations can also offer encounters with many species of sharks. Essentially this is a spectator sport: divers are positioned in a semicircle and sit in stunned awe as large groups of Caribbean reef sharks come in and take bait from the experienced shark wranglers dressed in chain-mail suits. Whether you agree with the practice or not, the baiting of the various sharks is the only way that you will have any kind of worthwhile encounter. Once the nurse shark and Caribbean reef shark were the most commonly seen species on these occasions, but now blacktip sharks, lemon sharks, and silky sharks join in the throng. In the last few years a number of new and exciting shark dives have been researched and divers are now able to experience action with oceanic whitetip sharks off Cat Island, bull sharks off Walker's Cay and Bimini, great hammerhead sharks also off Bimini, and, at the top of the food chain, the tiger shark—the apex hunter in these warm waters—which can be found around 25 miles (40km) off the northeast coast of Grand Bahama Island on a shallow bank, now referred to as Tiger Beach.

Grand Bahama

UNEXSO (The Underwater Exploration Society) situated at Freeport on Grand Bahama island is one of the oldest and longest established scuba diving centers in the Bahamas. With 30 years experience in the business, UNEXSO pioneered the first shark-feeding program and helped to dispel many of the myths that Hollywood wanted us to believe. There is daily shark feeding out at the **Shark Junction**, just ten minutes boat ride from the dock. A detailed lecture is given before each trip and divers are made aware of the risks involved with hand-feeding large wild animals. On first entering the water, you are positioned in front of an old upturned shipwreck. As the shark feeder arrives with a container full of fish, she is soon surrounded by snapper, grouper, horse-eye jacks, amberjacks, stingrays, nurse sharks, and predominantly Caribbean reef sharks (Carcharhinus perezi). Safety divers position themselves at the edges of the group and the shark feeder dressed in a chain-mail suit controls the action with the bait being kept in an enclosed PVC tube. Having had several years of acclimatization, the sharks now rush in and out of the feeding area, taking the bait from the shark feeder's hand. In some cases, she will stroke the sharks, particularly the larger females. These sharks not only react to feeding, they also love the tactile sensation of being stroked by the shark feeder.

OPPOSITE: Spectators are requested not to touch the sharks and to keep their hands tucked in as a safety precaution.

Grand Bahama is also home to one of the best wrecks in the Caribbean, the ship referred to as "Theo's Wreck." A former freighter, **MV *Island Cement*** was sunk in 1982 just off the South Beach Inlet. Lying on her port side in 100ft (30m) of water, she is now completely encrusted in coral and sponge growth. There are always large schools of fish surrounding her and at night the colors are simply amazing with much of the hull covered in brilliant yellow cup corals. Sleeping parrotfish and small shrimp are everywhere, as are lionfish.

Off Grand Bahama island lies the renowned **Tiger Beach**. From the Grand Bahama Bay Resort's marina it takes over an hour to reach the shallow sandbar referred to as Tiger Beach. Once the bait box is placed into the water and some "chum" splashed over the sides of the inflatable boat, several lemon sharks (*Negaprion brevirostris*) are likely to show up. Caribbean reef sharks will also show interest in the heavily chained bait box. Tiger sharks (*Galeocerdo cuvier*) may also appear and begin patrolling the area. This is the apex predator in warm waters and with its large blocky frame, short snout and forward-facing black eyes, you get the very distinct feeling of being closely watched.

New Providence Island

Possibly the greatest variety of shark encounters are located south of Nassau, the capital of the Bahamas on New Providence Island. Here at Stuart Cove's Dive South Ocean there is controlled feeding, but the excitement is particularly high when you first enter the water as part of a two-tank dive trip to the **Shark Wall** and **Runway**. A number of distinct types of shark dive are offered. At Shark Wall, divers enter the water on the lip of the oceanic trench known as the Tongue of the Ocean which drops 6,000ft (1,800m). Here there are at least a dozen resident Caribbean reef sharks and several large grouper which will accompany you on your dive along this spectacular coral wall. On the second dive, the shark feeder leads you a short way in from the lip of the wall into a wide sandy natural amphitheater. Here, dressed in either a full chain-mail suit or a minimum of chain-mail sleeves and gauntlets, the sharks are fed by means of bait attached to the end of a polespear.

The Nassau dive operators also have a much freer encounter with sharks, particularly silky sharks (*Carcharhinus falciformis*). This smaller pelagic shark is encountered 40 minutes after leaving the dock at Dive South Ocean where there is a United States

ABOVE: The tiger shark is the apex predator in the warm waters of the Caribbean and can be encountered at a dive area known as Tiger Beach northwest of Grand Bahama island.

Naval Buoy which is used to track their submarines. The buoy, which is some 20ft (6m) in diameter, has created an miniature open ocean ecosystem: the undersurface is covered by a film of algae which attracts small fish. Other species such as jacks and trigger fish seek shelter under the buoy and prey on the fish; these in turn attract larger and more efficient predators—the sharks. Such a favorable area for sharks was quickly discovered by fishermen and soon local dive operators saw the financial potential of attracting tourists to enjoy one of the most exhilarating diving experiences in the world.

Fact file Bahamas

BEST TIME TO GO
Like all of this area of the western Atlantic and Caribbean Sea, hurricane season is from June to November. The best encounters with hammerhead sharks are in February each year. Caribbean reef sharks can be seen all year round. The winter months can be more unsettled, but overall when the conditions here are perfect, it is stunning.

UNDERWATER VISIBILITY AND TEMPERATURE
Visibility is usually around 80ft (25m) on most dives with obvious periodic changes due to offshore storms or cloudy weather. The average water temperature is also variable due to the shifting eddies from the Gulf Stream and can range between 72°F (22°C) and 85°F (29°C). A full wet suit and hood are usually recommended, not only to keep you warm, but also to offer protection against abrasions and stinging particles in the water column.

Gulf of Mexico

Walker's Kay

Tiger Beach • Grand Bahama

Freeport City
Shark Junction • MV *Island Cement wreck*

Fort Lauderdale

USA

THE BAHAMAS

Great Abaco

Miami

Bimini Islands

New Providence Island

Nicholl's Town

0   100 km
0   50 miles

Andros Island

Runway • Nassau

Andros Town

Shark Wall

Bimini

Another shark encounter can be enjoyed at Bimini near the Bimini Sands Resort. A small shallow area just 1 mile (1.6km) outside the marina's entrance plays host to several large nurse sharks (*Ginglymostoma cirratum*) with their attendant remora fish and a handful of great hammerhead sharks (*Sphyrna mokarran*) patrol the sandbar for food scraps. The great hammerhead is the largest member of this subgroup and grows to a maximum length of 20ft (6m). It is often described as a danger to humans, although records of specific attacks are extremely rare. These large sharks are bottom feeders, swimming close to the seabed and "vacuuming" up any dead fish scraps, the

ABOVE: The blue parrotfish (*Scarus coeruleus*) spends around 80% of its time searching for food, scraping algae and small organisms from rocks with its beaklike mouth.

OPPOSITE: Great hammerhead sharks were once referred to as a danger to humans, but new research done by Stuart Cove has identified an area where these amazing sharks will swim freely among divers and snorkelers in only 20ft (6m) of water without posing a threat.

sand particles passing out through their gills. The experience of being in the water with these sharks is truly exhilarating. Free divers are also able to dive down and swim with these curiously shaped sharks which may feed in only 20ft (6m) of water.

"These large sharks are bottom feeders, swimming close to the seabed and "vacuuming" up any dead fish scraps ..."

Turks and Caicos

Atlantic Ocean

The Turks and Caicos group of around 30 islands are located 575 miles (925km) south of Miami and due east of two islands called the Inaguas. They are geographically aligned with the Bahamas and were formed at the same time. Only eight of the islands are inhabited. Set on two huge submarine peaks with a deepwater channel between them, Grand Turk to the east is 30 miles (48km) from the main Caicos group. Once renowned for its salt pans, it was part of the original Bermuda Triangle, a triangle of trade routes carrying salt to Bermuda in exchange for other goods traded with merchants on the east coast of the United States. Grand Turk is pretty laid back with some fine small hotels converted from old colonial homes, but for divers the main attraction is the vertical wall that drops into the abyss. Starting very close to the shore, you can dive the wall after just a short swim from the shore, but most divers use a boat for convenience. South on Salt Cay, which is a UNESCO World Heritage Site, are the remains of **HMS *Endymion***, a twin-decked sailing warship that ran aground in August 1790. Well broken up amid the shallow reefs, her 44 guns, various anchors, and other ship's parts are clearly visible scattered across the seabed.

Providenciales

Provo, as this island is known, lies to the west of the main Caicos group. Although still quite small, it is twice the size of Bermuda. It is here that most of the recent development has taken place and in some areas it can be quite reminiscent of Florida, with its multimillion dollar resorts and high-rise tourist hotels. While this island may not suit everyone, the diving is exceptional and should not be missed.

West Caicos

A mere 40-minute boat ride across the shallow lagoon to the south will bring you to the much less commercial West Caicos. Here the wall is simply outstanding and it is a firm favorite with underwater photographers as it starts in only 40ft (12m) and

LEFT: Tiny, multicolored Christmas tree worms inhabit many of the hard corals. They will disappear from sight in an instant whenever you get too close to them.

BELOW: Divers always love the drop-off of West Caicos with its vertical wall, starting in shallow water and dropping precipitously into the abyss.

drops precipitously. It is cut with numerous fissures and canyons. Good quality corals and plenty of fish are always seen here, as are turtles and eagle rays. The numerous underhanging ledges are covered with an algae fuzz that is grazed upon by wrasse, snapper, and grunt. Black coral and red rope sponges are common further down the reef and these are surrounded by large stove-pipe sponges, gorgonian sea fans, and numerous other soft and hard corals including whip-thin wire corals. If you look closely at these, you may see a tiny shrimp which spends its entire life on this species of coral. There are a number of dive sites all along this western wall and there is usually only a slight current flowing. It carries the nutrient-rich waters of the Gulf Stream to feed the islands' abundant coral reefs.

Because the Turks and Caicos are the very tips of ancient submarine mountains, wall diving can be enjoyed around the perimeter of all the islands. In a number of locations, the reef also has an inner shallow lagoon and here you can find eel gardens in the shallows, lots of conch and stingrays, and usually very clear water. Small coral heads, sometimes referred to as patch reef or "bommies" by Australians, are a natural oasis for life and play host to a larger than average selection of invertebrate species.

BELOW AND OPPOSITE: The Turks and Caicos group of islands have long been renowned for their spectacular walls and healthy reefs filled with colorful sponges and black corals, but these are also now home to many invasive lionfish.

Fact file Turks and Caicos

BEST TIME TO GO
The hottest months are September and October, but this is also hurricane season. Most divers tend to opt for April to June when the resorts are quieter and the sea and general weather conditions are more settled.

UNDERWATER VISIBILITY AND TEMPERATURE
Visibility is usually over 100ft (30m) and can be even better when you are along the outer walls. Water temperature is variable, ranging from around 82°F (28°C) in the summer to a pleasant 73°F (22°C) in the winter. You usually only need a light wet suit for all types of diving, irrespective of the time of year.

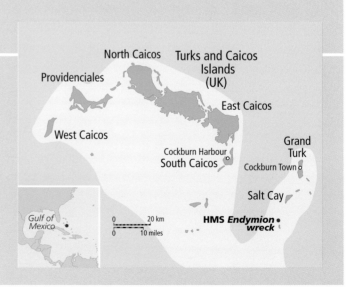

Atlantic Ocean and Mediterranean

Brazil

Atlantic Ocean

The Angra dos Reis region of Brazil, near Rio de Janeiro, features a large sheltered bay with a wide and diverse number of dive sites. Although the fact is little known outside its national boundaries, slowly word is getting out that the diving in Brazil can be exceptional. Ilha Grande, an island off the coast at Angra dos Reis, has curiously shaped rocky outcrops absolutely covered with golden cup corals (*Tubastrea coccinea*). The water temperature is quite cool—around 70°F (21°C)—so either a full semi-dry with hood or even a dry suit is recommended if you are going to spend any time in the water. Depths are only around 40ft (12m). These reefs are great for exploring and finding octopus, spiny lobster, and squid. There are signs that the invasive algae *Caulerpa taxifolia* has found its way here and this is worrying as it has taken over many areas of the Mediterranean too, and will kill off the slow-growing corals and sponges. Large grouper, Spanish hogfish, and hawksbill turtles are common as are many species of wrasse.

The Panamanian cargo ship **MV *Pingüino***, built in 1947, foundered here in June 1967. Completely open in aspect, her holds are quite cavernous, but easily negotiable with plenty of exits. The wreck sits in 60ft (18m) and is a protected marine reserve. The superstructure is covered in small scrubby corals, flower corals, low encrusting sponges, and many different species of algae, and there are usually plenty of small fish around her. Visibility is not that great—it is reminiscent of conditions in more northernly European waters, except warmer!

Fernando de Noronha

Perhaps the best diving is in the region known as Fernando de Noronha. This small island is the largest of the 20 or so in an archipelago on top of an ancient seamount. It lies 220 miles (350km) northeast of Natal on the northeast Brazilian coast, with flying time being around two hours from either Natal or Arecife. Once used as a penal colony, the island was declared a UNESCO World Heritage Site in 2001 along

RIGHT: Fernando de Noronha Island is a UNESCO World Heritage site in Brazil. The archipelago here lies a long way offshore, and is home to many endemic species.
BELOW: The corvette V17 *Ipiranga* sank accidentally in 1983 and the wreck is now covered in resident marine life and surrounded by many different species of fish.

with nearby Rocas Atoll. The reason was because the waters are important feeding grounds for billfish, various cetaceans, turtles, and large numbers of resident dolphins. Hawksbill turtles (*Eretmochelys imbricata*) also nest here and are usually seen on most dives. Overall the marine life is spectacular and there are regular sightings of manta rays, several species of moray eel, large grouper, and spinner dolphins, around 10,000 of which inhabit the area. The fact that it can support such a large population of cetaceans is testimony to the wealth of the marine life here. There is a nice mixture of both Caribbean and Atlantic species of fish including snapper, garden eels, and various angelfish and butterflyfish.

The **Caverna da Sapata** is a popular site with a superb vertical rock wall ending in a large cave which is easy to negotiate and explore. Stingrays are usually found on the sandy seabed here and a couple of grouper will probably accompany you during the entire dive. Although this rocky coastline lacks corals and can be fairly drab in color, the fish and encrusting species on the wall are always brilliant. With a maximum depth of around 90ft (17m), it is easily dived and the chances of seeing nurse sharks, rays, and eels are extremely high.

To the northwest of the island can be found the wreck of the corvette **V17 *Ipiranga***. At 160ft (56m) long, this Brazilian warship was built in 1953 and sank 30 years later in 1983. Sitting intact and upright in a maximum of 210ft (62m), the depth to the wreck is 150ft (46m) so time is limited, but the water is usually very clear allowing you plenty of time to explore the ship. Completely covered in cup corals, low encrusting sponges, and brilliant green algae, the ship's cannon are a delight. Surrounded by plenty of fish, this is a great dive and not to be missed. **Pedras Secas** or the Dry Stones are located almost due east of the most easterly point of the island and have an average depth of around 50ft (15m). They are well known for frequent sightings of large grouper, sharks, and turtles. Current should be expected on this offshore site so remember your surface marker buoy when ascending.

BELOW AND OPPOSITE: The Caverna da Sapata site is very popular with divers as it is so full of large friendly grouper, stingrays, and many colorful species of invertebrate.

Fact file Brazil

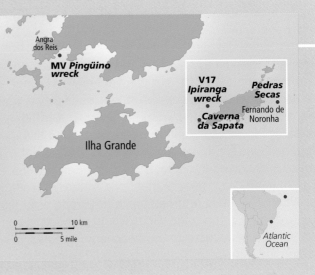

BEST TIME TO GO
The climate is tropical, with two well-defined seasons. The rainy season lasts from March to August; the best diving is done from September through January.

UNDERWATER VISIBILITY AND TEMPERATURE
Visibility is usually variable from 40–80ft (12–25m) around the mainland reefs, but this does get better out in the archipelago, where it will average over 100ft (30m). The water temperature averages 80°F (27°C) all year round, but a full wet suit is usually recommended to protect against abrasions and stinging things in the water.

Angra
dos Reis
MV *Pingüino* wreck
**V17
Ipiranga
wreck**
**Pedras
Secas**
**Caverna
da Sapata**
Fernando de
Noronha
Ilha Grande

0   10 km
0   5 mile

*Atlantic
Ocean*

Bermuda

Northwestern Atlantic Ocean

At the northern end of the "triangle" which bears its name, Bermuda is located around 650 miles (1,040km) west of Cape Hatteras in the United States and 3,750 miles (6,000km) from mainland Europe. This small subtropical archipelago of more than 150 islands in the northwestern Atlantic is linked together atop a vast submarine mountain. At one time, Bermuda would have been a fairly substantial island, before the level of the sea rose with the melting of the polar ice caps. Created by the formation of a gigantic volcano which rises some 15,000ft (4,500m) from the seabed, the islands themselves are the lower southeastern end of a former gigantic atoll. Could these islands once have been the fabled Atlantis reputed to be found beyond the Pillars of Hercules?

Situated surprisingly close to the North American coastline, and not in the Bahamas as so many people think they are, Bermuda lies on the same latitude as Dallas, Texas and is due north of San Juan in Puerto Rico. As they are virtually isolated in the northwestern Atlantic, you might expect the winters to be quite severe here, but fortunately for the Bermudas and their visitors, they are bathed in the warm waters of the Gulf Stream. Bermudians do not experience winter as such; it does get colder and wetter which keeps the islands a lush semitropical green, but Bermudians never see snow.

The Bermudas or *Bermudez* were originally claimed for Spain by navigator and explorer Juan de Bermudez around 1511, but it is not known whether he set foot on *Islas Demonios*—the Isles of Devils as the archipelago was known to the Spanish. Graffiti certainly indicates human presence at around this time because there are two initials, a cross, and the date 1543 carved into a rock which the Bermudians call Spanish Point, near Spittal Pond Nature Preserve.

When Columbus returned home to Europe after his first expedition, the trade winds would probably have carried him fairly close to the treacherous shores of Bermuda. It was probably just good fortune that prevented him from ending up alongside the other 300 or 400 ships which have sunk amid the reefs and shoals which surround these islands. These reefs are true coral reefs and are the most northerly coral reefs in the world. They are a three-tier system, comprising the outer large platform reefs and two inner circles which have almost completely surrounded the islands. Small wonder, then, that there are so many wrecks—and small wonder, too, that the diving is so good.

The main water areas around the islands are Great and Little Sounds leading into Hamilton Harbour, St. George's Harbour, on the north side of the airport, and Castle Harbour at the Causeway, where a number of islets stop the ocean swell coming into the sand flats. One of these is Nonsuch Island where the American naturalist William Beebe carried out some of the earliest deepwater experiments in a diving bell. Last but not least is Harrington Sound, a massive inland sea fed only through a narrow gap at **Flatts Bridge** where the tidal race can reach up to 4mph (6.5kph). However, at slack water the shore diving under the bridge is probably the best on the islands.

Flatts Bridge is certainly one of the best diving sites in the area as there is easy access, plenty of colorful marine life including spiny lobsters, moray eels, and the Bermuda blue angelfish (*Holacanthus bermudensis*) which is a subspecies of the queen angelfish found elsewhere in the Caribbean. Once the current picks up again, you can whisk under the bridge on the outgoing tide, and the current will deposit you in the marina where sea horses and frogfish are found regularly. The richness of the biodiversity at this site is such that the Bermuda Aquarium is also situated at Flatts Bridge. It is interesting to make a comparison between the species in the aquarium and the same species in their natural habitat only five minutes walk away. When diving this location, it is sensible to ask permission at the Aquarium first

OPPOSITE: Divers often encounter large numbers of tarpon (*Megalops atlanticus*) among the caverns and swimthroughs in the outer "breakers," the world's most northerly coral reefs.

and important to be aware of fishing boats and small passenger craft which constantly move in and out of the sound, particularly the research boats attached to the Aquarium and the Marine Biological Centre.

Notable shipwrecks

There are a huge number of historic shipwrecks that are well worth exploring, and there are also several ships that have been sunk deliberately as artificial reefs in prime sites to attract more fish and extend the interest of the nearby reef. They are well worthwhile visiting, as they are very photogenic and now well encrusted with all manner of marine growth. One of the best is the **Hermes** sunk in 1985 off Warwick Bay. Mooring buoys have also been placed at all of the prime sites to avoid damaging the reef.

Two of these wrecks in particular have such a great history that they inspired Peter Benchley's novel *The Deep*, the movie of which was largely made in Bermuda. The older of the two wrecks is the **Nola**, a paddle steamer which ran the blockades during the American Civil War. She ran aground in 1863. Bermuda was particularly active in the supply of all manner of goods for the war, from munitions to rum. This shipwreck is incredibly photogenic and you are able to explore large parts of it safely. Covered with a profusion of small knobby brain corals and purple sea fans, it makes a great backdrop for photography.

Easily explored on the same dive is the **Constellation**, a Second World War supply ship sunk in 1943 while carrying, among other things, cement and medical supplies including thousands of drug ampoules (the basis for Benchley's storyline). These are considered a great find by divers, but are in fact worthless as the drugs inside them have lost their potency over the years. Nearby is another wreck, the **Lartington**, which is incredibly photogenic and lies spread out in shallow water.

Other notable shipwrecks are the **Mary Celeste** which was also a Confederate blockade runner that hit the reef near the Sonesta Beach Hotel on September 6, 1864. Her great paddle wheels are still visible though now covered with all manner of coral growth. Other excellent wrecks include the **Minnie Breslauer**, an English steamer that sank on her maiden voyage on January 1, 1873, the **Darlington** wrecked February 21, 1886 en route from New Orleans to Bremen carrying a cargo of cotton and corn, and **L'Herminie**, a 60-gun French frigate wrecked on December 3, 1838 bound for France from Havana, Cuba. The brigantine **Caesar** was lost nearby in 1818, carrying a cargo of grindstones, clay pots with masonic markings, and glassware. One of the most photogenic wrecks is the largest ship ever to have been wrecked in Bermuda: the **Cristóbal Colon**, a 10,600-ton Spanish passenger liner that sank in October 1936 while bound from Cardiff in Wales to Veracruz in Mexico.

One of the most memorable of the southwestern reef dives is out at **South West Breaker**. This huge coral head breaks the surface and is known as a "boiler." The coral head is cut by a cave and tunnel system that runs all the way through it. Depth is about 46ft (14m) and visibility is usually in excess of 80ft (25m). This reef acts like a magnet for a myriad of fish, from angelfish to barracuda. Soft and hard corals, as well as purple sea fans, can be found

Fact file Bermuda

BEST TIME TO GO
The best time to visit the islands is mid-April to June and October to November. There is intense humidity at the height of the summer and the chance of strong winds caused by the various hurricanes that sometimes push up the eastern seaboard of the United States.

UNDERWATER VISIBILITY AND TEMPERATURE
Bermudian waters—by scientific measurement—are the clearest in the western Atlantic with 65ft (20m) underwater visibility being considered poor and 200–330ft (60– 100m) underwater visibility the norm on the outer reefs. Water temperatures range from 63–79°F (17–26°C).

Atlantic Ocean · Cristóbal Colon wreck · Eastern Blue Cut · St George's Harbour · Nola wreck · Constellation wreck · Lartington wreck · Castle Harbour · Darlington wreck · Harrington Sound · Flatts Bridge · L'Herminie wreck · Hamilton · Great Sound · Hamilton Harbour · Bermuda · Caesar wreck · Little Sound · Warkick Bay · South West Breaker · Hermes wreck · Mary Celeste wreck · Minnie Breslauer wreck · 0 5 km · 0 3 miles

everywhere. The **Eastern Blue Cut** is another favorite. It features caverns, lobster, and huge schools of silversides and queen parrotfish well out to the northwestern reaches of the outer rim of the atoll. It is often visited while diving the various wrecks in the vicinity.

Bermuda is still very much "that earthly paradise" first discovered and settled by Admiral Sir George Somers in 1609. This is one of those island locations where first impressions last forever. These are warm friendly islands with warm friendly people, exotic perfumes in the wind, color everywhere, small white-roofed houses next to pink beaches, the sound of

ABOVE: The *Nola* ran aground in 1863 and was a source of inspiration for Peter Benchley's book *The Deep*. Lying next to the Second World War wreck *Constellation*, both vessels can be visited on the same shallow dive.

kiskadee birds, and the singing of the tree frogs at night. It promises sailing over a turquoise sea, seeing the colors of the fish flash by, parasailing along South Shore, and exploring all those undived reefs and wrecks. Take a chance; you will not be disappointed.

Newfoundland

Northern Atlantic Ocean

Newfoundland is the most easterly province of Canada and in fact Cape Spear is the closest point to Europe. It is accessible by relatively short direct flights from Europe and the United States. If you gauge a vacation by the amount of flying time in relation to the cost of the vacation, divided by the potential for excitement and the possibility of fairly simple underwater photography, then Newfoundland rates very high indeed in the resulting league table of attractive destinations.

Divers who know the Oban area off the Scottish west coast generally agree that one of the best wrecks of all time is the Swedish-registered *Hispania* which struck Sgeir Mor in the Sound of Mull on December 18, 1954. Well … Bell Island in Newfoundland has the equivalent of four *Hispanias*. All of the ships are intact and sitting upright in a maximum depth of 92–130ft (28–40m).

Bell Island is the largest of the three islands in Conception Bay, located to the northwest of St. John's, the provincial capital of Newfoundland. The island was once one of the primary suppliers of iron ore to the Allies during the Second World War, but all of her underground mines are now long since flooded. However, the island's real claim to fame came from a couple of brief but costly encounters with German U-boats in 1942 when Newfoundland became the only place in North America where a direct attack on land installations was undertaken by the German navy. On two separate occasions U-boats stole into Conception Bay, sank two iron ore carriers and also blew up the main pier on Bell Island.

The wrecks

In September 1942, the *U-513*, a Type IXC oceangoing German submarine commanded by Rolf Rüggeberg, made her way undetected into the massive Conception Bay inlet. On the morning of September 5, Rüggeberg struck with deadly force using his boat's torpedoes to sink the SS *Saganaga* and the SS *Lord Strathcona* while they were lying at anchor, before escaping into open waters and the safety of the North Atlantic.

RIGHT: Colorful sun starfish and sand dollars litter the seabed amid northern sea urchins, flounders, and spider crabs.
BELOW: Giant eelpout over 3ft (1m) long are the primary predator in the shallow waters around southern Newfoundland, where they feed on small crustaceans and other fish.

The iron ore carrier **SS *Saganaga*** was 410ft (125m) long and had a gross tonnage of 6,012 tons and was at anchor in Lance Cove when she was hit. Now lying in 112ft (34m) on an even keel, her main deck is in 75ft (23m). There is a massive gaping hole amidships and the wreck, like the other three in this cove, has suffered top damage from the occasional iceberg which drifts through the sound and gets snared on the superstructure. Imagine a dive on a nearly intact ship dating from the Second World War with an iceberg on its deck stretching to the surface and beyond—incredible!

The **SS *Lord Strathcona*** was struck on that same morning and now lies in 120ft (36m) with her main deck at 90ft (27m). At 460ft (140m) long and weighing 8,085 tons, it takes several dives just to explore the upper deck of this ship. Better preserved than the *Saganaga*, the main superstructure is completely open and easily negotiated without hindrance, except for the time to depth limitation. All of the holds are open and, with care, exploration can be undertaken inside the ship. There are some fishing nets snagged onto the structure, so great care must be taken.

Two months later, on November 2, the *U-518* entered Conception Bay as a slight detour on the way to Quebec where a spy was offloaded. With the knowledge of his colleague's previous success, Captain Friedrich Wissmann approached Lance Cove and sank two more ore carriers, the SS *Rose Castle* and the *P.L.M. 27*.

The ***Rose Castle*** was also 460ft (140m) long and weighed 8,601 tons. The deepest of all the sites, the ship sits in 130ft (40m). Again, the ship is upright, making her upper decks in around 92ft (28m) perfect for exploration. Due to her greater depth, the ship is more intact than the others and is considered the best preserved of all the ore carriers.

The last of the four ships sunk that night off Bell Island, the ***P.L.M. 27***, was a Free French vessel. She was 404ft (123m) long and weighed 6,209 tons. Her initials stand for "Paris Lyon Marseilles" and she is by far the most accessible of all the ships. Ocean Quest Adventures have placed two safe mooring lines with buoys on her, one at the stern and the other at the bows to allow you to explore the ship safely over a number of dives. With her deck in only 66ft (20m), she has sustained the most iceberg damage, but she is perfect for extending your time after exploring her intact propeller and rudder. The seabed is littered with debris amid a field of scallops, mussels, flounders, ocean pout, and burrowing anemones and starfish.

OPPOSITE: The wrecks in Conception Bay are literally covered in giant green and white plumose anemones. Large lumpsuckers (or lumpfish) have also made these wrecks their home as these rotund fish have few natural predators here. The males look after the egg brood until they hatch.

These four ore carriers are possibly the best modern warships that you will ever dive—and that includes those in Scapa Flow. The water is cold, ranging from 32°F (0°C) at the seabed to a balmy 57°F (14°C) at the surface, quite a change and certainly a welcome relief as you hang out on the mooring line degassing on the way back to the boat.

Marine life

The marine life in these northern Atlantic waters is very like that found in British waters: there are similar species of kelp, bladder wracks, winkles, and huge scallops. The wrecks are absolutely smothered with large green, orange, and white plumose anemones and soft corals, with every bit of metal space covered. Lumpsuckers (*Cyclopterus lumpus*) are common and found all year round. Commercially harvested for their roe which is exported to the Baltic States, they abound all over the wrecks. The starfish and most nudibranchs are of the same type as found in British waters and even the wolffish are the same species. But the wolffish in these northern waters compete in the ugly stakes with the ocean pout (*Macrozoarces americanus*). This is a type of eelpout which has grown to massive proportions, usually over 3ft (1m) long; they have a similar sized head to the wolffish, but no obvious teeth, only massive fleshy lips!

There are hundreds of flounders all over the seabed which is also home to sand dollars (a type of flat sea urchin) and large moon snails. Skate are common in shallow waters and the predominant local species of fish is undoubtedly the variation of the wrasse family called a "cunner" (*Tautogolabrus adspersus*). Very similar to corkwing wrasse, these are more spotted and equally as nosy as their British cousins. Cod are everywhere as there is no commercial fishing allowed for the species without a license to catch individual fish.

Diving really doesn't get much better than this: the lure of snorkeling with whales combined with icebergs and pristine Second World War wrecks is just spectacular and thoroughly recommended.

Fact file Newfoundland

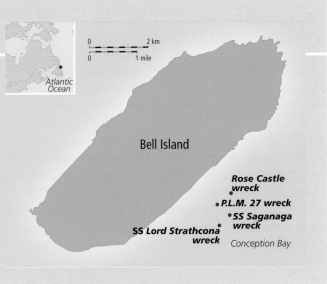

BEST TIME TO GO
In May and June you may still find icebergs that have broken away from the pack ice and come into Conception Bay. June is great as the water is still clear enough to enjoy the wrecks and is really starting to warm up. The diving around Bell Island has large numbers of eelpout, flounders, sand dollars, and wrasse.

UNDERWATER VISIBILITY AND TEMPERATURE
Visibility is variable, but usually around the 50ft (15m) region to allow you great vistas of the wrecks. A deep halocline at around 100ft (30m) leads to temperatures at 32°F (0°C) on the seabed, yet rising to 57°F (14°C) on the surface. You need just enough time to defrost before the next dive!

Atlantic Ocean

0   2 km
0   1 mile

Bell Island

Rose Castle wreck

P.L.M. 27 wreck

SS Saganaga wreck

SS Lord Strathcona wreck

Conception Bay

Azores

Atlantic Ocean

Located in the mid-Atlantic, the Azores comprise nine islands and lie around 930 miles (1,500km) west of mainland Portugal. Geologically they are relatively young at less than 1 million years old. The nine islands and their satellite rocks and offshore seamounts form an archipelago that measures 906sq miles (2,346km^2) in surface area. Volcanic in origin, most are mountainous, very verdant, and incredibly scenic. They are reached by direct flights via Funchal in Madeira to São Miguel, the largest of the Azores islands. All of the islands have their own airstrips, but many dive boats travel around the main triangle of Faial, Pico, and São Jorge. Originally colonized by the Portuguese in the mid-15th century, their natural position is their best strategic asset and they are still regarded as the most important mid-ocean refueling point for yachts, ocean cruise liners, and commercial shipping.

Faial is dominated by an ancient volcano and its crater. It is often referred to as the Blue Island because of the blue-colored hydrangeas which bloom there in summer. Untouched by mass tourism, the islands are perfect for scuba diving and have built up an enviable reputation for encounters with sharks, manta rays, sperm whales, and many other cetaceans.

Faial

The Azores' position may mean that they are on a migration route for sharks, but the presence of sharks is more probably caused by cold water upwelling which attracts huge quantities of fish species to the seamounts on which the large populations of sharks feed. Blue sharks (*Prionace glauca*) and shortfin mako sharks (*Isurus oxyrinchus*) are the most commonly seen. Like all "prearranged" shark encounters, the water is "chummed" first to bring them in. Shark diving off Faial is located about an hour's boat ride southwest of **Capelinhos Volcano** to the **Condor Bank** seamount. The blue sharks are usually about 6.5ft (2m) long and are generally inquisitive, coming right up close to divers. Several usually turn up at the same time and they are quite approachable. Shortfin

"The blue sharks are usually about 6.5ft (2m) long and are generally inquisitive, coming right up close to divers."

RIGHT: Turtles are commonly seen on the offshore seamounts, so while looking out to see the big game fish, always remember to keep an eye out above you for the turtles.
BELOW: Blue sharks are found on several offshore seamounts and they are attracted by "chumming" the water with bait, which brings them close to the divers for the best encounters.

Fact file Azores

BEST TIME TO GO
Due to its latitude along the Mid-Atlantic Ridge, the Azores experience a generally average, subtropical climate, with mild annual oscillations. Daily maximum temperatures usually range between 59°F (15°C) and 77°F (25°C). It can get windy and wet and the weather is affected by the periodic, yet fairly predictable, tropical storms that cross the Atlantic. June to September are the best months when you will have most chance of seeing the large pelagic visitors on the offshore seamounts.

UNDERWATER VISIBILITY AND TEMPERATURE
The Gulf Stream raises the sea temperature to about 68–73°F (20–23°C) during the summer months and the visibility is usually around 80ft (25m), and certainly much more than this around the seamounts. Full wet suits or semi-dry suits are recommended as well as warm clothing for the boat trips when diving offshore.

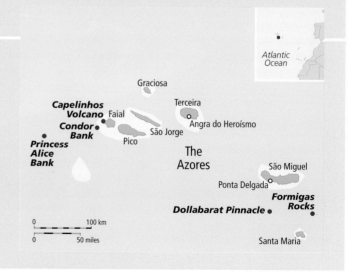

Atlantic Ocean

Graciosa

Capelinhos
Volcano Faial

Condor
Bank

Princess
Alice
Bank

Terceira

Angra do Heroísmo

São Jorge

Pico

The
Azores

São Miguel

Ponta Delgada

Formigas
Rocks

Dollabarat Pinnacle

0   100 km
0   50 miles

Santa Maria

makos are much faster moving and they often arrive suddenly out of the blue depths, scaring the smaller blue sharks away. Usually only six divers are allowed in the water at any time.

Offshore seamounts such as the **Princess Alice Bank** are superb for wild creature interactions, usually with manta rays, dolphins, large tuna, barracuda, and various jacks. *Mobula* rays are often seen here. It really is pot luck regarding the species that will turn up, but you will certainly see something extraordinary. This submerged mountain is located 58 miles (93km) southwest of Pico Island and rises from over 1,000ft (300m) to within 115ft (35m) of the surface. It requires a long boat ride of over three hours to get there and conditions are not always calm!

Other great dives around São Miguel include **Formigas Rocks** about 20 miles (32km) offshore and nearby **Dollabarat Pinnacle** which is great for seeing big tuna and barracuda. It comes to within 13ft (4m) of the surface. It can be choppy, but the rugged pinnacle walls are surrounded by fish, including several species of bream. Black coral can be found here and there are regular sightings of turtles and manta rays.

Dive sites range from steep vertical walls to gentle sloping cliffs and the rocky seabed; volcanic in origin, the rocks are covered with scrubby algae which is home to several species of nudibranchs, starfish, and anemone. Bream, damselfish, triggerfish, parrotfish, moray eels, and several species of grouper are usually on hand as are stingrays, spiny lobster, and a number of species of shrimp. The Azores also offer more than the offshore seamounts and encounters with big pelagic fish and cetaceans—all levels of diver can enjoy fantastic diving closer to their island base and some even offer shore diving.

ABOVE LEFT: Curiously shaped caves and caverns are common here and the marine growth on the rocks is very interesting with all manner of fish and invertebrates to be found.
LEFT: Manta rays are just one of the many large oceanic pelagic fish that are encountered regularly in the Azores.

Scapa Flow
Northern Atlantic Ocean

There is always a sense of mounting excitement as you approach the Orkney Islands situated 15 miles (25km) north of the Scottish mainland. The first huge land mass that looms up out of the early morning mist is the island of Hoy and the ferry lands at Stromness, where you disembark directly next to the harbor where most of Scapa Flow's fleet of diving boats is based. Most of these are converted fishing trawlers, and their skippers and crew are incredibly experienced in the history and diving of these sunken vessels.

This cold, deep, formidable natural harbor has served military fleets for centuries. Many ships have been scuttled here, but most of them have been salvaged. At present there are still three German battleships, four light cruisers, five torpedo boats (destroyers), a Second World War escort boat (*F2*), two submarines, 27 large sections of remains from salvage operations and salvors' equipment, 16 known British wrecks, 32 blockships, and two Royal Navy battleships (the **Vanguard** and the **Royal Oak**). A further 54 ships are as yet unidentified.

German fleet wrecks

Considered by many to be impregnable to attack, the bay of Scapa Flow covers some 120sq miles (310km²) and is completely sheltered by a ring of protective islands. At the end of the First World War, the German fleet surrendered, was taken into internment, and set sail for Scapa Flow, the home of the British Royal Navy. It is easy to imagine the consternation of the locals in November 1918 when the ships of both the Royal Navy and the German High Seas Imperial Fleet steamed into Scapa Flow. Over the winter months, the relations between the Allies and the interned German crews deteriorated and most of them were repatriated to Germany.

The fate of the German fleet was being negotiated at the Treaty of Versailles, but on June 21, 1919 the German commanding officer Admiral Ludwig von Reuter became convinced that war conditions were about to be reinstated and that his fleet would be seized by his country's enemies to be used against his homeland. He had not been informed that the negotiation period to conclude the Treaty had been extended. When the British fleet left that morning on exercise after seven months of confinement, von Reuter decided to save his countrymen's honor and deliberately scuttled the fleet. At 11 a.m. the skeleton crews on board opened condensers, valves, and pipes. Within four hours, most of the ships had sunk from view, many turning turtle on their way down to the seabed. Others were beached.

Sinking the Royal Oak

Some 20 years later, on the night of October 14, 1939, the 600ft (188m) battleship HMS *Royal Oak* lay at anchor in the sheltered bay of Scapa Flow. Her duties were to protect Kirkwall and the British fleet from aerial attack. Scapa Flow was considered impenetrable because of the narrow passages between the reefs and islands. Any attack was expected only from the skies. However, nobody told this to the commander of the German submarine *U-47*, Günther Prien, who stealthily approached Scapa Flow in what is considered by many to be one of the bravest feats in naval history. At the dead of night, he attacked and sank the *Royal Oak*. The vessel is now a designated war grave and is protected by Navy Law, so diving on her is strictly forbidden.

Diving the wrecks

Most of the diving in Scapa Flow is technically demanding and virtually all of the German fleet wrecks should be treated as potential decompression dives. Not only does this put a lot of stress on the diver, it considerably reduces the time that can be spent in the water and the ultimate enjoyment of the wrecks. Many divers are attracted to the technical side of deep diving, but the need to attend courses and buy

OPPOSITE: The shallow blockships are perfect for all levels of diver as they are located in clear, clean water. They are covered with marine life and perfect for photography.

❝Most of the diving in Scapa Flow is technically demanding and virtually all of the German fleet wrecks should be treated as potential decompression dives.❞

the equipment must be considered. Furthermore, the larger battleships are not only in very deep water, they are all upside down. Unless you want to spend your entire dive on the underside of a ship's hull, you will have to explore further around the vessels, but remember that this can be dangerous.

Thankfully the best diving and underwater photography is undertaken on the shallower wrecks. The German light cruiser **Karlsruhe II** is a perfect example; lying on her starboard side in only 85ft (26m) of water, she is perfect for exploration. Her classic rounded stern and anchor are evocative reminders of this great age of warship construction. The other light cruisers **Cöln**, **Brummer**, and **Dresden** are also excellent while perhaps the best of the battleships is the **Kronprinz Wilhelm**—her massive guns offer divers a wonderful opportunity to see the main armament of a dreadnought-era battleship.

The blockships

Apart from the German warships, other wrecks include the blockships **Dyle**, **Gobernador Boreis** (known locally as the "Goby"), and the upside down **Tabarka**. They are all found at the westernmost entrance of Burra Sound so these dives are dictated by the state of the tide, as they can only be done at slack water and on an incoming tide, due to the ferocity of the current. These wrecks are all in under 60ft (18m) of water and while it would be good to spend more time on them, the increasing speed of the current means that only around 35 to 45 minutes is possible before you are whisked off and you have to free your delayed surface marker buoy to indicate your position to the following dive boat so that it can pick you up.

In between dives, the dive boats often anchor on the jetty at Lyness, the former naval base on the island of Hoy where there is a museum with an excellent display of artefacts relating to the two World Wars. Nearby is the wreck of the **F2**, a German escort vessel captured in the Second World War, and her salvage barge, which sank in 1968. The salvage company had just removed a set of guns from the F2 and had tied tight onto the stricken vessel (at low tide). The crew then went off to celebrate their good fortune at being able to raise the guns and left their trophy to a rising tide. Lo and behold, their barge (and their booty) promptly sank. They now make two very nice diveable ships (both with guns)—the wrecks are attached by rope.

Scapa Flow undoubtedly offers the best wreck diving in Europe and certainly ranks in the top five in the world. The history and drama which have unfolded here over the years is testimony to the importance of the area, which is now designated under the Protection of Wrecks Act. All are considered National Monuments and it is an offense to tamper with them.

OPPOSITE: Ballan wrasse (*Labrus bergylta*) are very common on the blockships and will follow divers around as they are extremely curious and always on the lookout for tidbits.

ABOVE: Divers explore the underside of one of the shallower wrecks. The shallow depth allows plenty of time to explore them fully from kelp-covered bow to anemone-covered stern.

Fact file Scapa Flow

BEST TIME TO GO

April to October are usually best due to the warmer water temperature and more ambient light. Once November comes, the depth of the water means that every dive seems like a night dive as it is so dark. Scapa Flow is virtually an enclosed sea and unless the weather is particularly atrocious (as can happen) you can dive at any time or state of tide.

UNDERWATER VISIBILITY AND TEMPERATURE

Visibility is variable and as this is almost an enclosed sea, the particulate in suspension in the water can take ages to settle. Consequently the average is around 20ft (6m), but it can easily climb to over 80ft (25m) which is superb on the larger shipwrecks as you can get a very real idea of the scale of the warships. Temperature ranges massively from 36–61°F (2–16°C).

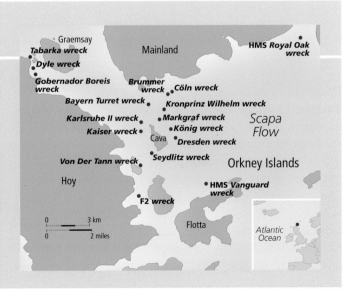

St. Abbs and Eyemouth

Northern Atlantic Ocean

In the southeast corner of Scotland, just a short boat ride from the English border and near the famous Farne Islands, lies the first voluntary marine reserve in the British Isles, which was founded by myself in 1984. This area of the Berwickshire coast is now recognized as having the greatest diversity of marine life around the British Isles. The topography combined with the lack of significant freshwater river runoff and the direct influence of both the North Atlantic Drift (an offshoot of the Gulf Stream) and a tail from the colder Arctic region have created an area quite unrivaled anywhere else. Both cold-water and warm-water species are found living quite happily alongside one another.

Marine conservation has been important around St. Abbs and Eyemouth since the time a voluntary ban on the removal of shellfish was first imposed by divers in the early 1970s. Many diving clubs supported this move. The first real change came in 1978 when I established a small area to the north of Eyemouth as a voluntary marine reserve. Barefoots, as it was then known, is still a major part of the St. Abbs and Eyemouth Voluntary Marine Nature Reserve, which was founded in 1984 and officially opened by Professor David Bellamy in 1986. Located just 7 miles (11km) north of the English border, the reserve now extends from the Hurkar Rocks at Eyemouth to St. Abbs Head. It includes 4 miles (7km) of coastline and extends out to the 165ft (50m) depth contour.

Voluntary Marine Nature Reserve

There is an almost total lack of "diver pollution," except at one or two of the most popular sites, and then only during peak vacation times. This is due to the infrastructure available, such as good road and rail links, plentiful accommodation of various types and standards, equipment sales and hire, boat hire, launching facilities, compressors, wrecks, good photographic opportunities, etc. The dives within the marine reserve range from easy, gently sloping shore dives to challenging drift dives that are undertaken in difficult tidal conditions.

RIGHT: Rocks covered with the soft corals '"dead men's fingers" and topped with kelp are synonymous with the marine reserve.
BELOW: Lobsters are commonly encountered on every dive and are plentiful, prospering because of their protected status within the marine reserve.

The seabed is generally covered with large boulders falling away to gravel and sand at about the 65ft (20m) zone. The exposed cliff faces are renowned for the great diversity of marine life and are festooned with "dead men's fingers" soft corals, brilliantly colored anemones, hydroids, tunicates, fish, and crustaceans. On these cliffs ballan wrasse (*Labrus bergylta*) eat out of your hand, while wolffish try to eat the rest of your hand! The predominant feature is the kelp forest which fringes much of the coast, grazed by sea urchins and home to spider crabs, nudibranchs, and two-spot blennies. Further offshore are brittle-star beds with giant dahlia and plumose anemones, the rare Arctic *Bolocera* anemone, burrowing anemones, and huge angler fish. Octopuses and squid are common on night dives and the rare Yarrel's blenny isn't considered rare here—it is found among the gullies, canyons, and caves which cut through the headlands.

Shore diving here is just as popular as boat diving and in fact most visitors will make their first dives directly from a number of safe shore locations. At Eyemouth a steep set of steps to the north of the town gives direct access to a natural canyon called **Weasel Loch**. From here divers can get to a number of very rewarding sites including Divers Hole, the Canyons, and Little Leeds Bay. To the south of the town is Green Ends Point which has its own parking area and access down an old concrete pathway (once the top of an old wastewater outlet). From here you can enter the sea at any state of the tide; as there is a 20ft (6m) tidal range here, that is no mean feat for a site that offers easy shore access.

Eyemouth harbor

A huge number of boat dives leave Eyemouth harbor marina and the offshore wrecks, left over from the two World Wars, are now internationally recognized as some of the best diving in Europe with freighters, armed carriers, German U-boats, and many other vessels. While these sites are a focus for more technical divers, probably 90% of all diving takes place in the shallow coastal waters that can be accessed by all levels of sport diver.

A number of shore dives are available directly off the harbor's protective wall at St. Abbs village, with the best of all being **Cathedral Rock**. This huge underwater archway has a smaller arch above it known locally as the Keyhole. The walls and the roof of the arch are festooned with a dwarf species of the plumose anemone as well as sponges, soft corals, mussels, and hydroids. Large numbers of friendly ballan wrasse can be seen. The site is a popular destination for television film crews who know that the abundance of marine life found here is highly indicative of the entire North Sea species diversity.

Numerous day-diving boats take divers to St. Abbs Head which is a National Nature Reserve. Topped with precipitous cliffs and home to hundreds of thousands of seabirds in the breeding season from May to August, the spectacular scenery on top is complemented by the terrain underwater. There are caves, caverns, swimthroughs, soft coral-encrusted boulders topped with vibrant kelp plants, cliff faces festooned with all manner of marine invertebrates— all surrounded by schools of fish. Sites such as the Barnyard, Skelly Hole, Anemone Gardens, Tye's Tunnel, and Wuddy Rocks are internationally admired. The local shipwrecks here are also well worth exploring and are all in under 100ft (30m) of water.

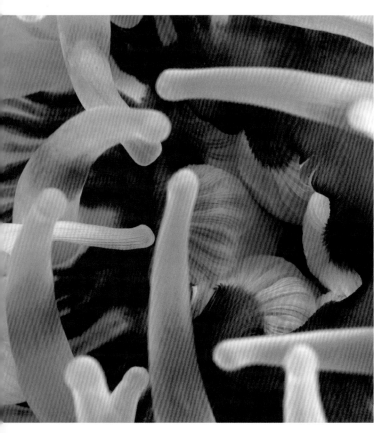

LEFT: Brilliantly colored dahlia anemones are found all over the rocky substrate and can be seen in a multitude of hues.
OPPOSITE Schools of silvery sandeels come in close to shore to breed in the spring and summer. They are a vital link in the food chain in this marine environment.

Fact file
St. Abbs and Eyemouth

BEST TIME TO GO
Undoubtedly the best time is from April through to October to avoid the worst of the winter storms that pile in across the North Sea. This area of the coastline is fairly exposed and diving can often be blown out, so it is sensible to check the forecast before setting off to dive.

UNDERWATER VISIBILITY AND TEMPERATURE
Visibility is usually favorable due to the fact that there are no major river runoffs along this stretch of coastline. Average visibility is around 50ft (15m). Temperature ranges widely from 36–61°F (2–16°C).

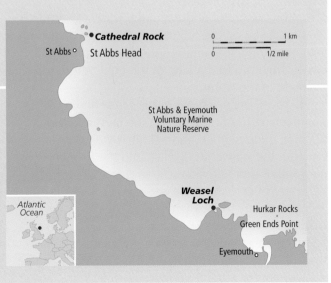

Cathedral Rock
St Abbs   St Abbs Head
0   1 km
0   1/2 mile
St Abbs & Eyemouth
Voluntary Marine
Nature Reserve
Atlantic
Ocean
Weasel Loch
Hurkar Rocks
Green Ends Point
Eyemouth

Farne Islands

Northern Atlantic Ocean

The Farne Islands are a small group of some 33 rocks and islets that are located off the north Northumberland coast of England. At high tide, only 23 of the larger rocks and islands are visible, but all of them are eye-catching. The entire group are a National Trust-protected area and have numerous wildlife preserves, notably for seabirds and seals. There are more than 50 historic shipwrecks around these islands, but it is principally the encounters with grey seals that bring divers and underwater photographers back time and time again to this picturesque group of islands that lie just less than 2 miles (3km) offshore.

There are numerous sightseeing boats and dive boats which run regular trips to the islands but in the opinion of many divers Paul Walker of Farne Discovery has the most experience of and empathy with the seals and the best knowledge of the hidden shoals, wrecks, reefs, and currents, which can play havoc with inexperienced divers and boat skippers.

Diving with seals

Depending on the rising and falling tide as well as current conditions, Paul Walker takes small groups of divers on his boat *Farne Discovery* to the best locations for two dives. Seals are everywhere; there are often hundreds of them in the water, all of them looking at you on the bright orange boat. The younger yearlings and subadults are the most curious, often coming right up to the side of the boat before you even get in the water.

However, once you are in the water and approaching the first seals on the surface, they become quite skittish and will quickly disappear beneath the waves and vanish into the kelp-covered canyons. Swimming slowly, it pays just to stay still midwater or crouch on the seabed and wait for the seals' curiosity to overtake them. They just cannot help themselves and soon come right up to you and seemingly pose for the camera. As seals can slow their heartbeat down while underwater, they can stay submerged for around 15 minutes and often appear to be asleep on the seabed or amidst the shallow kelp. This is just a ruse to ambush you; while you are "sneaking" up to photograph the resting seal, another seal will circle behind you and may start to tug at your fins, or even try and pull your dive hood off! As soon as you turn around to confront your attacker, it scoots off or just stays in midwater acting all innocent.

The seals clearly have enormous fun doing this and the mood gets quite infectious, as the divers enjoy the experience just as much as the seals. The Farne Islands are one of the best and safest locations for in-water encounters with one of the sleekest hunters in British coastal waters and the opportunity for diving with them should not be missed.

OPPOSITE: With thousands of seals in the colonies, diver encounters with the grey seal are common, reliably predictable and always a delight for both seals and divers.
BELOW: The Farne Islands, off Northumberland's northeast coast, are a nature reserve and home to thousands of seals and seabirds including puffins and terns.

Fact file Farne Islands

BEST TIME TO GO
From May through to October the juvenile seals are at their most inquisitive and will come right up to you. This area of the coastline is fairly exposed so some of the diving can be blown out, but the Farne Islands have so many lee shores and sheltered bays where the seals congregate that good encounters are usually guaranteed.

UNDERWATER VISIBILITY AND TEMPERATURE
Visibility is usually favorable because there are no major river runoffs along this stretch of the coastline. Consequently average visibility is around 50ft (15m). Temperature ranges hugely from 36–61°F (2–16°C).

Longstone

Longstone Lighthouse

Harcars

Wamses   Blue Caps

Brownsman

Gun Rock   Staple Island

The Pinnacles

Staple Sound

0 ———— 1 km
0 ———— 1/2 mile

Atlantic Ocean

Cornwall

Northern Atlantic Ocean

Who would have thought that Cornwall in southwest England would become one of *the* shark diving regions in the world? From May to July large numbers of migrating basking sharks pass near the British coast feeding on the vast quantities of plankton that drift past Land's End and continue up through the Irish Sea and then up the west coast of Scotland. These basking sharks (*Cetorhinus maximus*) migrate up the coast each year, feeding as they go. Little is known about these sharks. There are claims of some being 50ft (15m) long, but more commonly 14–20ft (4–6m) specimens are encountered. Like other similar species of sharks, they are thought to be ovoviviparous (where the fertilized eggs develop within the female before the young are born live). The gestation period can be as long as three and a half years. Males possibly mature at around seven years, but again so little is known of this species and its habits that such estimates are really only guesswork.

Basking sharks and blue sharks

The main area for seeing basking sharks in Cornwall is off Penzance, as that is where most of the shark watching businesses operate from. These huge creatures are first sighted on the surface, the tips of their dorsal fins and long tail slicing through the water with sometimes their long pointed snout also clear of the surface, a very good indicator that the shark is feeding. Visibility can be very variable but these are the conditions that the sharks like best as they are solely plankton feeders, consuming the minute larval fish, copepods, crustaceans, and other tasty critters. They are the second largest shark, behind the whale shark (*Rhynchodon typus*) which is the largest fish in the world. On entering the water on a dive, there is usually little to see at first, then slowly a gigantic cavernous mouth appears. Wide enough to swallow a diver whole, the shark will take little notice of any human observers and just continue to filter the plankton from the water passing through its massive gills at the rate of 2,000 tons of seawater per hour.

As the plankton bloom passes and more sharks appear, the water does get clearer and this makes for more exciting encounters. It is a huge effort to keep up with the sharks in the water and time spent in the boat to get you into position is of particular benefit so that you can position yourself directly in front of the sharks and minimize the swimming time needed to try and keep up with them.

Later on in the season, another opportunity presents itself when blue sharks appear in the coastal waters, but several miles offshore. As with other shark encounters, like in the Bahamas for instance, baiting does take place to bring the sharks close to the boat. Once more, you are only snorkeling—no scuba is involved. Hands and head have to be covered and as the water is fairly cool, a full wet suit, sem-dry, or even a dry suit is recommended to allow you the comfort of spending a reasonable time in the water.

The blue shark (*Prionace glauca*) is a species of requiem shark and is found worldwide, preferring temperate waters of around 45–61°F (7–16°C). Living as far north as Norway and as far south as Chile, this shark also likes to spend time around the shores of the south coast of England during July and August to feed on the squid and cuttlefish which congregate there. They give birth to live young, bearing 25 to 100 pups at one time and often congregate in large numbers. To have any interaction with these sharks, the water also has to be "chummed" (baited with a mixture of blood and fish carcasses). Once you enter the water wearing full wet suit, hood, and gloves, you stand the chance of a truly wonderful one-on-one experience with a wild animal. Make no mistake, these types of encounters are not for the fainthearted and should be treated as potentially dangerous, like all shark encounters.

Fact file Cornwall

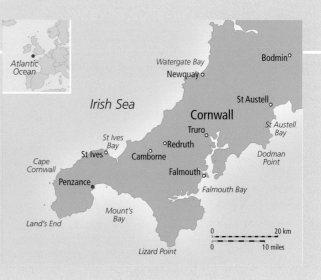

Medas Islands
Mediterranean Sea

Along the northern Catalan coast of Spain are found the Islas Medas (Medas Islands), which lie fairly close to the vacation resort of L'Estartit. The largest of the group of around nine islands is Meda Gran which is topped by an old 19th-century lighthouse. The Catalan Autonomous Government declared the Medas Islands a national marine protected area back in 1983. Thankfully those early measures have not only protected the species found around the islands, they have also helped to encourage the diversity of marine organisms and fish to be found in the region. The protected zone not only includes the rocks themselves, but also important *Posidonia* seagrass beds where large noble pen shells

(*Pinna nobilis*) live. Large grouper fish inhabit the many caves along the coast here and this is an important breeding ground for many species of sea bream, dentex, sea bass, and wrasse.

Tame grouper are now found on every dive amid the caves and caverns of the Medas Islands. Large schools of anchovies, sardines, jacks, and even bonito and barracuda are encountered here as well as cow rays and small stingrays. The runoff from the River Ter to the south of the reserve carries nutrients which help the marine species to thrive here. An ocean current also brings cooler nutrient-rich waters from the deeper Mediterranean and this combination of natural features make these islands very special.

Mooring buoys are permanent fixtures on the dive sites to minimize any possibility of damage and divers have to pay a small fee to help finance the running and maintenance of the reserve—a worthy investment. Now hundreds of divers descend on L'Estartit weekly and although it sometimes appears that the harbor is full to capacity with dive boats and their passengers, there is more than enough space for everyone.

Cova del Dofi Sud (Dolphin South Cave) is found at the entrance to one of the complex of caverns that are sculpted around the island of Meda Petita. A small stylized statue of a dolphin stands at the main entrance. Hardly inspiring as statues go, but the cavern walls are covered with tiny yellow cup corals, red coral branches, and numerous hydroids and bryozoans. Schools of various species of bream can be found in all the caverns and caves and small cleaner shrimp, slipper lobster, and spotted nudibranchs abound in the crevices.

LEFT: Schools of bream are often encountered in the caves and caverns of the Medas Islands where they feed on sea urchins, crustaceans, and smaller fish.
OPPOSITE: Large grouper (*Epinephelus marginatus*) are what divers come to see in the Medas Islands. These huge friendly fish will almost certainly accompany you on every dive.

The cavern is simply massive at over 165ft (50m) long and has several sculpted exits on the south side. The overall dive time needed to explore all the chambers can exceed one hour and the maximum depth reaches 80ft (25m). What does surprise most divers, however, is the number of huge friendly grouper; many have been hand-fed over the years (although this practice is now frowned upon) and the grouper are so unafraid of divers in the water that they often follow you around like puppy dogs.

Weighing 225lb (100kg) or more, they can be quite intimidating and often sneak up behind you when least expected.

Further large caverns are found on all the other islands, and in fact all along the limestone coastline of the Costa Brava. Most, as yet, are still unexplored. This is truly spectacular diving and it gives a rare insight into a dark world rarely seen by others. Many of the caves have air chambers where stalactites are to be found when you explore them.

Another popular dive is **Pedra de Déu** at the northeastern point of Meda Gran. There is a deep cavern in 140ft (42m), but everyone swims to the corner of the island where a small rocky spur sits clear of the surface of the water. Underneath this rocky outcrop is a vertical wall which has numerous small shafts and tunnels eroded through the soft limestone substrate. Accompanied by large friendly grouper at every tunnel, the dive is excellent for fish photography. In the deeper crevices tiny slipper lobsters abound and small striped shrimp act as cleaners to the resident population of grouper.

A nearby wreck, the **Reggio Messina**, is also popular, but it is well broken up near the natural arch of **Roca Foradada**. However, it lies in 105ft (32m) and visibility is such that you will very rarely see the whole wreck. This former ferry was deliberately sunk in 1992 by the maritime authorities to provide a new attraction for visiting divers. In the same vicinity is the **Avvenire** —often referred to as the *Marmoler* as she was carrying a cargo of marble mezzanine floor tiles. The 165ft (50m) long freighter crashed into the Montgri coast in 1971, slid backward, and eventually sank in 138ft (42m) of water. Located 2 miles (3km) off the coast, visibility is very variable and can sometimes be as low as 13ft (4m). There are a couple of underwater thermoclines and the water temperature really drops as you descend to the superstructure. The first thing you notice are the clouds of anthias goldfish. All of

the metal parts are covered with a patina of algae and hydroids, soft small sea fans, and sea squirts. As the wreck is quite deep, dive time is limited. With bad visibility, the experience is like having a cold night dive with little to see.

Caves, tunnels, and seamounts

The entire coastline stretching north to the border with France is very reminiscent of Malta and Gozo with massive vertical limestone bluffs cut by numerous caves and caverns. Some of them are visible from the surface but others can only be guessed at underwater. Las Vetas is first and has at least five different exits. At one point there are three very obvious openings leading to the sea, but a number of small side caverns always lure you away from the light to search for tiny shrimp and slipper lobsters. El Mila is even larger and has numerous air chambers where stalactites are still being formed, the air redolent with the stink of thousands of bats! The Tunel de la Pedrosa is another favorite at an average depth of 80ft (25m). The tunnel is completely straight, over 230ft (70m) long, and very wide and high. It traverses the headland and the experience is superb as you emerge into the open sea. The walls are covered with all manner of small corals and sponges.

Traveling south down the coast there are a number of seamounts which rise to within 17ft (5m) of the surface and a very interesting mix of marine life can be found, including tiny jewel anemones. The sides are covered with purple and yellow sea fans, many of them playing host to small winged oysters and the egg cases of dogfish. The usual bream and sardinella are everywhere, as are chromis and anthias. A similar haven for marine life is Canyons de Tamiru which are three fingers of limestone rising from 150ft (45m) up to 30ft (9m). The walls are smothered with gorgonians and the narrow channels just funnel schools of fish through them as the diver swims forward. This is a spectacularly scenic dive, and also superb for marine life photography.

The Mediterranean is too easily written off as lacking fish and marine life. The conservation policies put in place for the Medas Islands back in the early 1980s have paid off handsomely. Not only are the islands and their marine life fully protected, the overspill of the fish and crustaceans that breed in the region have allowed for a sustainable fishing industry to grow and of course have allowed scuba divers to revel in some of the best diving to be found anywhere in the Mediterranean.

OPPOSITE: Large burrowing tube anemones come out at night and use their long tentacles to catch passing prey.

ABOVE: A diver focusing on the larger grouper swimming among the islands often overlooks the beauty to be found in the smaller marine life, such as this golden cup coral.

Fact file Medas Islands

BEST TIME TO GO
The months of May through to October are usually favorable with fair offshore winds and generally calm seas. The caverns have to be dived with little or no surge but the Medas group all have lee shores, so there is always somewhere sheltered to get into the water. Some current should be expected around the rocks and on the deeper wrecks.

UNDERWATER VISIBILITY AND TEMPERATURE
Visibility is usually around 60ft (18m), but can easily be over 100ft (30m) in the caverns as it is so still. Temperature drops as low as 54°F (12°C) in the winter, but in the warmer months it can be around 65°F (18°C). This is not exactly balmy so it is recommended that a full wet suit or semi-dry suit plus hood should be worn for comfort.

Malta, Gozo, and Comino

Mediterranean Sea

Set amid the sparkling southern Mediterranean Sea, the Maltese archipelago lies some 58 miles (93km) south of Sicily and 288 miles (455km) from the African coast. Geographically and politically isolated, the Republic of Malta consists of three main islands and a number of smaller satellites. The three main islands, Malta, Gozo, and Comino, are not only steeped in history, they are home to an incredibly diverse range of marine life and some of the most scenic diving to be encountered in the world.

At first sight, the islands seem dry and barren, but they are incredibly fertile and support a thriving agricultural industry. The tiny bays are filled with brightly colorful "luzzu," the traditional Maltese fishing boat, often used to ferry tourists around the islands. The language is a curious mixture of Arabic, English, and Latin, known as Malti. Due to their geographical location, the islands have been conquered many times by many nations and the language reflects this rich cultural heritage.

The Maltese islands are one of the top diving destinations in the Mediterranean, popular with German, Dutch, Italian, and British divers, with currently around 50,000 divers visiting each year. The islands are undergoing a resurgence in popularity and new conservation policies are being spearheaded to meet international demands.

The majority of diving is done by visiting independent divers and clubs. Once you have your Maltese Diving Permit, there is virtually no limit to the number and type of dives that are open to you. Deep diving is an obvious attraction and a number of the offshore wrecks are very popular with technical divers. Malta has long been considered one of the most popular Mediterranean destinations, but many divers don't realize that much of the best diving is actually done on Gozo, with day-trip cars and dive center vehicles crossing several times daily on the ferry. The island of Comino lies between Malta and Gozo and can be seen to the east as you pass by on the ferry. Famous for its shallow bay known as the **Blue Lagoon**, the island is very popular with locals. Comino also has some very interesting dive sites where the concentrations of fish life are, if anything, higher than around the other islands (even if only due to the level of tourist-driven fish feeding which goes on).

Malta

Of the three islands in the group, Malta is by far the largest, and it is here that the international airport is located. To get to Gozo you have to cross virtually all of Malta, then take the ferry to Gozo from Cirkewwa, which is soon to be designated a Voluntary Marine Reserve. It will be the first of its kind on the islands, and is one of the top shore diving sites on Malta. With easy parking and ease of access, the reef drops off in steps down large algae-encrusted boulders to the seabed at around 80ft (25m). The wreck of the *Rozi* sits nearby and more experienced divers tend to include this at least once during their visit. The tugboat *Rozi* was deliberately sunk in 1992 as an attraction for the glass-bottomed boats that used to take tourists around this headland, but divers soon found her perfect to visit on an easy dive as she sits upright on a sandy bottom at 120ft (36m). The ship is now home to thousands of fish, with chromis, bream, and sand smelt being the predominant species. Nearby, the *Posidonia* sea grass beds are home to cuttlefish and pipefish.

Valletta Harbour

No stranger to war, the islands have been besieged many times over the centuries and were once home to the Knights Templar. During the Second World War in recognition of their perseverance and courage in the face of almost daily bombing runs by the German air force, the islands were awarded the George Cross for valor by a grateful British government which had its

OPPOSITE: A number of aircraft wrecks are dotted around the Maltese islands. They were shot down or crashed accidentally during the Second World War. These planes make for an interesting dive destination as they are now covered in brilliantly colored sponges and surrounded by fish.

main Mediterranean naval base in Valletta Harbour. Six ships were sunk in the harbor during that conflict. The most popular in terms of easy shore dives are HMS *Maori* and the *Carolita* barge. Many warplanes were also lost around the islands and these are slowly coming to light as more exploratory diving takes place around the coastline.

The **Blenheim Bomber** near Marsaxlokk to the southeast of Malta is now very popular, but its depth of 140ft (42m) dictates the experience of the diver that can visit and the consequent time penalties that apply at such depth. Located by Sport Diving Ltd, this Second World War aircraft lies approximately 2,600ft (800m) due east of Xorb Il-Ghagin, off southeast Malta. Most of the Maltese dive stores visit the site, but due to the depth and its offshore location they will only take experienced divers. Fairly intact, the wreck is about the only interesting thing in the area and sadly little time can be spent exploring it because of the problems associated with the depth.

The **Bristol Beaufighter** near Sliema is another popular attraction in 100ft (30m) of water. It is largely intact and upside down. There is little else to see on the surrounding flat sand seabed, but the wreckage is a mini-oasis of marine life. A number of former ferries have also been sunk as diver attractions and these

ABOVE: The Mediterranean seahorse is quite common in Maltese waters and can be usually be found in the Coral Cave at Dwejra on Gozo.

are slowly becoming encrusted with algae, various bryozoans, and small cup corals. Offshore, to the northeast of Malta, is a British submarine that is well worth visiting by more experienced divers. Now that there are full technical diving facilities on the islands, the deeper wrecks that sank in both World Wars are also now accessible.

Gozo

This island is about a quarter of the size of Malta, but is more popular with visiting divers as they are able to dive independently (with a Maltese Diving permit) without having to pay for boat hire to get to the reefs and wrecks of Malta. Undoubtedly some of the best diving to be done in Gozo is also by boat, particularly at **San Dimitri Point** where schools of barracuda are the norm. However, the majority of dives in Gozo are accessible directly from the shore—depending on their experience, divers can reach 200ft (60m) as a shore dive. **Xlendi Bay** and **Mgarr Ix Xini** are fantastic night dives in under 40ft (12m) of water and you will be pleasantly surprised at the amazing diversity of marine life to be found, including some species more commonly associated with the eastern Caribbean. Flying gurnards, golden conger eels, stingrays, sea horses, filefish, cuttlefish, and octopuses are all common here and the lights from the small café on the shore make a welcome sight after spending more than 90 minutes underwater.

The Mecca for divers on Gozo is at **Dwejra Point** —here divers flock to one of the natural wonders of the Mediterranean. Dwejra Point has a huge natural arch which juts out from the headland and connecting to this is a vertical slash through the cliff which is accessible from the sheltered bay surrounded by fisherman's huts known as the Inland Sea. Depths range from 80ft (25m) below underhanging cliffs, before dropping to over 200ft (60m). The sight of the azure water at the end of the canyon is simply awesome, but care must be taken with the depth here. If you do the dive shallow, you will have enough time and air to continue to your left and pass under the massive archway known as the Azure Window, before exiting the water at the Blue Hole.

This area of western Gozo is regarded by many as one of the top diving destinations in the Mediterranean with several fantastic sites found within a small area and all accessible from the large car lot. Walking over an ancient seabed now dotted with fossilized shells, there is easy access down to a natural wave-carved depression in the ancient sandstone. The outer edge

LEFT: The entrance to the Blue Hole at Dwejra is simply superb. From here you can access the Azure Window and the Coral Cave, where sea horses are found regularly. The nearby Inland Sea is on the same headland and it offers spectacular underwater vistas.

of this is very similar to the ironshore rocks of the Caribbean, but your view is dominated by the gigantic archway of the Azure Window.

On the shore side is the famous **Blue Hole** which has very easy and sheltered entry and exit points. After dropping down into the center of this hole, you will see a horizontal slab facing you and a huge natural archway underwater. To the left of the arch is a small coral cave which is well worth exploring as there are always tiny shrimp and conger eels there. Once under the arch and swimming further toward the corner, a thin fissure leads up to a narrow, very colorful chimney. Continuing along this vertical wall,

you will come to another huge underwater cavern known as the **Coral Cave**. The Coral Cave can also be reached from the shore, but the access point can be quite daunting as you launch yourself into the air before hitting the water directly above the entrance. But this way of getting into the water saves the long swim to the cave from the Blue Hole.

In the southwest and south of Gozo, the land mass rears up vertically, with few entry points except at Xlendi Bay. From St. Andrew's Divers Cove in Xlendi Bay, much of this coastline is explored by dive boat, which is the only way to get to the caves below these awesome ramparts, particularly toward the Ta Cenc Cliffs which are incredible. In winter time the periodic rains can reduce visibility in the natural inlet at Xlendi Bay, but the boat dives are still superb. Over at Reqqa Point a vertical drop to 200ft (60m) is just another shore dive, but more spectacular is the **Blue Dome** at the entrance to the Ghasri Valley. Sometimes referred to as Cathedral Cave, this is one of my favorite dives. The cave is found along the right-hand wall, with entry in only 17ft (5m). Inside, there is a huge domed ceiling which reflects the outside light creating the "blue dome." Perfect for photography, the cave walls and rocky floor are filled with marine life including pen shells and sea horses.

Fact file
Malta, Gozo, and Comino

BEST TIME TO GO
Diving is commonly done all year round as there is always a lee shore and plenty to see. The wide variety of historic shipwrecks, aircraft, and artificial reefs attract a fair share of enthusiasts who enjoy technical diving. The weather in May to October is usually more settled and since much of the diving is directly off the shore, there is little to stop you diving as often as you like.

UNDERWATER VISIBILITY AND TEMPERATURE
Visibility is usually around 80ft (25m) or more on all dives at any time of the year and often even better. The temperature is variable, although warmer than other Mediterranean sites due to a fairly constant stream of warm water which passes around the islands. The average is around 64°F (18°C).

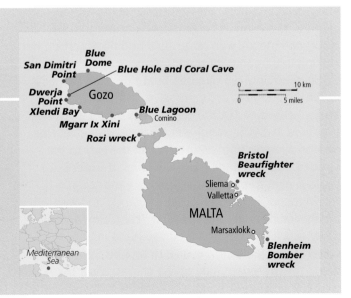

Cyprus

Mediterranean Sea

Located in the eastern part of the Mediterranean a long way southeast of Greece, Cyprus has long been a diving haven for European divers who have enjoyed its warm, clear waters for many years. There are no amazing coral reefs here, but rather massive boulders covered in scrubby algae, encrusting sponges, and tiny cup corals. These rocky reefs are usually home to plenty of octopuses, starfish, and numerous species of wrasse and bream. The best dive by far is on the former Ro-Ro ferry *Zenobia*. It is classed as one of the top wreck-diving sites in the world. When you fly into Larnaca airport, you can usually see the shipwreck from the air as the water is generally fairly clear outside the harbor.

The ship was built in Sweden in 1979 but sank off Larnaca on her maiden voyage to Tartous in Syria in June 1980. She was loaded with more than 100 articulated lorries plus general cargo including food, cigarettes, and eggs (which can be seen on the seabed) for the eastern Mediterranean countries. A problem occurred with the computerized pumping system to her ballast tanks and she started to list heavily. The ship was towed out of the harbor to prevent any obstruction to other shipping and when her list got progressively worse, she was refused entry back into port. She capsized taking with her over $300 million of cargo. Legend has it that the insurance money was never paid and no report on her sinking has been published.

Located only ten minutes boat ride from Larnaca harbor, the ship is an impressive 584ft (178m) long and weighs over 10,000 tons. She now rests on her port side in 140ft (42m) and is simply massive. Her depths average from 52ft (16m) all the way to the seabed and, depending on your level of expertise, you are able to explore her various car decks and wheelhouse. Her propellers are gigantic and well worth visiting, with one found at 75ft (23m) and the other at 125ft (38m). Most divers tend initially to undertake a fairly simple dive to around 52ft (16m) along the starboard side of the ship to allow them to view the shipwreck and familiarize themselves with

ABOVE AND OPPOSITE: The ferry *Zenobia* is rated the number one dive wreck in the eastern Mediterranean for visiting divers.

what is available deeper down. The upper car deck and accommodation block are negotiable and there is always plenty of light to gain easy access and exit.

At 90ft (27m) are the canteen and bridge and they are easily negotiated, giving you a real sense of the scale of this massive shipwreck. A number of divers have been lost on the wreck over the years, and so if you are unsure of entering confined spaces, then please do not do so without having taken proper dive instruction. Make sure that you are accompanied by a very competent and qualified guide. Swimming underneath the trucks is not recommended as many are still only supported by their safety chains— weighing over 40 tons each, they will eventually break off and plummet down through the car decks.

The superstructure now has a patina of algae, small colonial bryozoans (which look a bit like hard corals), small cup corals, and tube sponges, and is grazed on by countless species of wrasse and sea bream. The water column often has barracuda and chromis in it and you should be aware that the deeper and darker recesses may have large grouper and moray eels. Large tuna and amberjacks are usually seen while exploring the wreck, as are kingfish, stingrays, triggerfish, and even turtles.

Fact file Cyprus

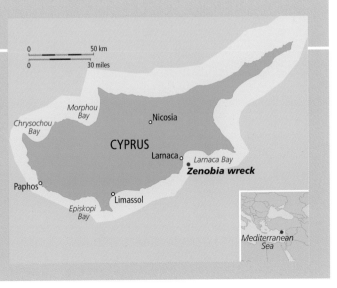

BEST TIME TO GO
Diving on the shipwreck is possible all year round. If you are unfamiliar with wrecks, it is sensible to perform a shallow orientation dive first before you explore further.

UNDERWATER VISIBILITY AND TEMPERATURE
Visibility is usually around 80ft (25m), but during May to October before the rainy season starts the visibility can easily exceed 165ft (50m). The temperature average is around 65°F (18°C), but can drop as low as 54°F (12°C) in the winter months when full semi-dry suits or dry suits are recommended.

Northern Red Sea, Indian Ocean, and Indo-Pacific

Northern Red Sea

Red Sea

The northern Red Sea is the closest tropical coral reef to Europe. Only a three- to four-hour flight away from most major cities in Europe, theoretically a European dive tourist could be there by lunchtime and underwater that same afternoon. The shores around the Sinai Peninsula and the coast south from Hurghada to Marsa Alam and beyond used to be much easier for shore diving, but now the massive tourism boom and the construction of vacation resorts means that much of the shore is out of bounds. As a result, you must use either day-dive boats or live-aboard dive boats. On the latter you can spend your entire vacation at sea and enjoy perhaps the best variety of sites, from wrecks to reefs, vertical walls to dolphin-infested shallows, where sea cows or dugongs may be seen. And every site that you visit in the northern Red Sea is just covered with the most brilliantly colored soft corals.

Ras Muhammad

Located at the very southern tip of the Sinai Peninsula, Ras Muhammad is a national marine reserve. It points directly south to the greater expanse of the Red Sea, with the deep Gulf of Aqaba to the east and the shallower Gulf of Suez to the west. There are a huge number of shipwrecks in these waters, and usually at least once a year a tanker or cargo vessel will misjudge the shallow reefs that lie just below the surface next to the major shipping lanes and run aground. Thankfully there is usually little damage to reef or ship, but over the years, particularly since the opening of the Suez Canal, there have been many shipwrecks which are simply magnificent to dive and explore as most of them are easily accessible in under 100ft (30m) of water.

Ras Muhammad is arguably one of the best dives on the planet. The reef wall starts just below the surface and plummets vertically and undercut into the abyss. A saddle of around 40ft (12m) connects three submarine coral heads where large Napoleon wrasse (*Cheilinus undulatus*) patrol. The outer wall of the larger reef is known as Shark Reef and it is superb

LEFT: The remains of the steamship *Kingston* up on Shag Rock are simply superb and covered with all manner of corals and surrounded by tropical fish.

BELOW: Distinctively colored coral grouper tend to hang out under colorful coral ledges, waiting to prey on the small fish that swim by.

Fact file
Northern Red Sea

BEST TIME TO GO
While some of the best diving is from March to September, the biggest schools of fish at Ras Muhammad are found in July and August. This virtually landlocked sea is dived all year round and no matter how windy it gets in the winter months, there are always sheltered bays with fantastic reefs and wrecks. Every month here delivers great diving. A full suit is recommended at all times, as the wind can be chilly, particularly after a long dive and a lengthy boat ride.

UNDERWATER VISIBILITY AND TEMPERATURE
Visibility is reduced around Sha'b Ali due to the surrounding shallow sand banks, but normally it is over 100ft (30m); unless you are diving at night, be prepared for some amazing vistas, particularly on the deep vertical walls. The temperature averages 75–79°F (24–26°C), dropping in the winter months to around 68°F (20°C).

with massive schools of emperor fish, barracuda, batfish, jacks, and usually a few sharks deeper down. The wall is spectacularly colored with brilliant soft corals, those ubiquitous golden anthias, red coral grouper, Picasso triggerfish, and lionfish. The smaller reef is now referred to as Jolanda Reef after the Cypriot cargo ship that came to grief there in April 1981. The smallest reef is known as the Tower and in between the three are masses of fish including huge moray eels, stonefish, and triggerfish.

To the east of Ras Muhammad is the Gulf of Aqaba and much of the commercial shipping that plies these waters passes through into the Gulf via the Straits of Tiran. This natural funnel of fast-moving water is created by the island of Tiran to the east and four submerged reefs atop an ancient limestone saddle, restricting the passage of boats and speeding up the tidal stream. These reefs from south to north are Gordon Reef, Thomas Reef, Woodhouse Reef, and Jackson Reef. Normally tackled as a day dive trip, the prevailing wind is from the northwest, so all the dive boats hang out on mooring lines at the southeastern corner, creating all sorts of confusion as there can be several dozen dive boats at any one time. Usually there are too many divers on any one spot, so it may be best to do these dives from a live-aboard which will allow you to dive all the areas of these reefs, far away from the madding crowd. The reefs are spectacular with huge gorgonian sea fans, black corals, brilliant sponges, turtles, tuna, barracuda, and more fish than you can imagine.

Sha'b Ali

Perhaps one of the most famous shipwrecks discovered in recent years is the **Thistlegorm**, a British Merchant Navy ship, which was bombed by the Germans during the Second World War when she was anchored in the maze of reefs known as Sha'b Ali. Apart from the stern where the main magazine was stored, the ship is still relatively intact, but what makes this wreck so special is that it was absolutely stuffed full of ammunition, spare aircraft parts, a Bren gun carrier, trucks, motorcycles, a railway steam locomotive, and just about everything

else in between. Her holds are completely open and easily negotiated. Vehicles and parts were stowed on several levels and they are now completely encrusted in a patina of marine growth. Friendly turtles, bannerfish, parrotfish, barracuda, angelfish, and lionfish vie for space amid shoals of glassy sweepers swimming through the colorful soft corals. Live-aboard captains often moor up overnight on the *Thistlegorm*, allowing you to do a late afternoon dive (after the day boats have left), a night dive, and a pre-breakfast dawn dive. This type of diving is absolutely spectacular and yields many different species of marine life not normally seen during the daylight hours.

Sha'b Ali is massive and unless you know the way through the shallow coral heads, it is easy to get disorientated. You understand why there are so many wrecks. The reef is very protected and home to a few other wrecks such as the **Dunraven**, while further north on Shag Rock are the remains of the steamship **Kingston**. The corals have grown over the ship's superstructure making her incredibly photogenic. Regular pods of wild dolphins (*Tursiops truncatus*) are seen here. In fact the entire western wall of Shag Rock is well worth exploring. Southwest lies Sha'b Abu Nuhas where you will be delighted to find another four major shipwrecks.

When I worked in the Red Sea in the 1980s, I witnessed the cargo ship **Giannis D** running aground in May 1983 and was one of the first divers to dive on her. A little further along this exposed northern edge of the reef are another two wrecks, the **Chrisoula K** and the **Kimon M**. *Chrisoula K* was a 322ft (98m), 3,720 ton Greek-registered freighter that struck a

OPPOSITE: Schools of batfish are always found off Shark Reef at Ras Muhammad, at the tip of the Sinai Peninsula.

RIGHT: Regal angelfish are just one of many different, brilliantly colored tropical reef fish that are found in abundance in the northern Red Sea.

coral reef in this part of the Red Sea in August 1981. *Kimon M* was of similar size and tonnage and she met her fate on the same reef in December 1978. Another, very old wreck (judging by her lines and coral growth) also lies here: the **Carnatic** was a ship belonging to P&O (the Peninsular and Oriental Steam Navigation Company) and she ran aground on this reef on her way to Aqaba in 1869, shortly after the opening of the Suez Canal. Sadly five passengers and 26 crew were lost and the wreck almost destroyed the company. She was extensively salvaged as she was carrying specie (coin of the realm) and copper ingots, but her holds still contained various bottles and artefacts. Unfortunately much of this has subsequently been plundered over the years.

OPPOSITE: Marsa Alam is renowned for its superb table corals, turtles, dugong, and superb seagrass beds.

BELOW: The *Thistlegorm* on Sha'b Ali is one of the iconic Red Sea dives. This is regarded as one of the best wreck dives to be found anywhere in the world.

The Brothers Islands

As you continue southwest from Hurghada to Marsa Alam you will encounter a huge number of hotels and dive resorts. Much of the diving here is done by boat, but it is probably easier to dive from a live-aboard. The Brothers Islands are located 70 miles (113km) offshore in the middle of the Red Sea and consist of two barren limestone outcrops which are the tips of an ancient mountain. The northern island (Big Brother) has a lighthouse on it manned by a permanent crew and two superb shipwrecks: the British cargo ship **Numidia** sunk in 1901 and the **Aida** sunk in 1957. The *Numidia* on her northern point is perhaps the most photogenic of all the northern Red Sea wrecks, stretching from the surface to over 260ft (80m) deep. Her spars and beams are heavily encrusted with soft corals. Surrounded by fish, this wreck is on most divers' Red Sea list. The smaller island known as Little Brother is deserted, but her subterranean reef spur extends to the south where there is a fair chance of seeing thresher sharks (*Alopias vulpinus*) and oceanic whitetip sharks (*Carcharhinus longimanus*).

The island's geographic isolation and the fact that it is swept by massive currents has ensured that the walls here have some of the best quality corals found anywhere in the Red Sea, particularly the simply massive forest of sea fans.

Directly south is another oceanic reef in the middle of nowhere. **Daedalus** barely breaks the surface, but can always be detected by the "boiling" of the water as the waves crash over this shallow coral reef that rises hundreds of feet from the seabed. Strong currents run along its flanks and care should be taken on this superb drift dive. You should dive all of this reef by tackling the easterly wall in the morning and the westerly wall in the afternoon to make the most of the ambient sunlight that illuminates the soft corals and anthias goldfish that surround you.

Inshore and west of Daedalus is Marsa Alam. This really isn't a place where you would vacation as it is simply a fishing village and embarkation point for Panorama Reef, Daedalus, and the superb **Sha'b Samadai**. Port Ghalib is where the main resorts are and Emperor Divers have a superb reputation in the area for day boat dives, as well as for extended trips to the southern reefs. The small marsas (or bays) indent the coastline and all have steeply sloping reef walls leading to large seagrass beds where huge green turtles feed and dugong come to have their young and feed on the seagrass. These bays are synonymous with gorgeous corals and interesting sights, such as huge numbers of citron gobies in the *Acropora* coral, massive table corals, and a very wide variety of angelfish and butterflyfish.

Maldives

Indian Ocean

Most visitors to the Maldives will never forget their first vision of this string of jewellike coral atolls as they descend into the airport at Malé. Those aerial views seem to epitomize the island chain as you soak in the deep indigo blue of the depths surrounding the clear turquoise waters of the shallow lagoons, ringed with palm-tree-dotted sandbars. Undoubtedly the islands are in danger from global warming and with the sea rising each year as the polar caps melt, they seem under increasing threat. However, this cycle of rising and falling sea levels has gone on for millennia so we can hope that the coral growth may just be able to keep up with the rising water.

The Maldives are joined geographically to the Lakshadweep archipelago to the north which belongs to India and continue southeast to the Chagos Bank, one of the largest protected marine regions in the entire Indian Ocean. More than 1,200 islands stretch across 539 miles (868km) of ocean ranging about a straggly string of 26 major atolls arranged in a north-to-south direction. The islands each have their particular charm. Most are uninhabited. They offer fantastic diving. Virtually all of the atolls also have *thila* (a local name for a submerged coral head) and much of the diving is concentrated around these reefs where raging currents can attract some of the largest marine creatures.

North Malé Atoll is the largest of the atoll systems and consists of hundreds of tiny islands and submerged reefs. There are more resorts here than anywhere else in the Maldives and this atoll is usually where most divers get their first taste of what is on offer here. In the middle of the channel between Boduhithi and Kudahithi can be found Boduhithi Thila. Largely exposed as the channel is so wide here, it is diveable during the northeast monsoon. Currents have to be expected on this *thila* when the incoming or outgoing tide is running.

While this *thila* has a good covering of small *Acropora* corals and colorful soft corals, it is the oceanic wanderers that come here to feed on the

plankton-rich waters flowing from the lagoon that are the main attraction. Divers can expect to see manta rays, whale sharks, jacks, emperorfish, barracuda, batfish, and grey reef sharks. The reef sides are covered with soft and hard corals where brilliantly colored red grouper and lionfish lie in wait for small golden anthias and chromis to swim within their reach. Picasso triggerfish, scorpionfish, bigeye, filefish, and coronetfish are common and while your eyes may wander to search out for the large critters, it is really the smaller creatures which are special on this great dive.

Rasfari Island in the south is an exceptional drift dive through a narrow channel that cuts through into the lagoon from the vertical outer reef wall. Always done on an incoming current to allow for safe boat pickup, divers can expect to see various sharks, large schools of jacks and tuna as well as several species of ray including mantas and eagle rays. Also in the southern region, but this time on the east, is Girifushi which is a marine protected zone. Expect masses of gorgeous soft corals surrounded by millions of colorful fish. This site so resembles some of the walls in the Red Sea that it is always fun suddenly to come across a species of fish that is definitely not found in the Red Sea, such as the clown triggerfish (*Balistoides conspicillum*) with its distinctive large white spots on the lower half of its body and brilliant orange lips, or the yellowmask angelfish (*Pomacanthus xanthometopon*).

Ari Atoll in the northern section of this string of atolls is one of the largest and consequently offers plenty of different types of diving. There are caves, caverns, vertical walls, drift dives, and probable encounters with grey reef sharks and manta rays.

The **Maaya Thila Protected Area** lies inside the lagoon of northern Ari Atoll. Like most marine conservation zones, it can get rather busy, particularly as the *thila* can be negotiated on a single dive. However, for those who love critter hunting, you will find leafy scorpionfish, frogfish, crinoids with attendant shrimp, leather corals with small cowries, and simply millions of brilliant orange cup corals which cover much of the underhanging ledges. If you have time on your dive and want to get away from the crowds, there are a couple of satellite coral heads which sit away from the main *thila*. These are well worth exploring; the site is often used for night dives.

All the atolls have their associated manta ray cleaning stations and to southwest of Ari Atoll can be found one that is quite special. **Manta Point** or Hukuruelhi Faru is found on the southern side of the

Rangali Channel. A natural bowl has been sculpted out and a huge coral cave lower down the reef is testimony to the fact that water levels were much lower in the past. There is a good variety of soft corals and sponges and tropical fish life is abundant over the whole site. However, it is the mantas that everyone comes for; although sightings are not guaranteed, there is a fair chance that you will spot at least two or three at the cleaning station.

Kudarah Thila Protected Area is located on the opposite side of the atoll and close to three major tourist resorts. Although the *thila* is divided into four large coral heads, the site is prone to really strong currents and is unsuitable for novice divers. It does get very busy, but usually the bottom time on the dive is limited so that divers are not around for that long. When you are underwater it doesn't appear crowded at all except for the fish life and the grey reef sharks which congregate near the point. With a maximum depth of around 135ft (40m) the coral heads rise to 40ft (12m) below the surface. Divers usually spend most of their restricted bottom time in the 60–80ft (18–25m) zone where there are huge undercut ledges full of caves and caverns. Whip corals stretch out into the current and small gobies can be seen on many of them. The entire area is just filled with brilliantly colored soft corals and reef fish and it is amazing just to drift with the current alongside them.

Located 95 miles (150km) from Malé are the twin atolls of **Nilandhoo** with **Faafu** in the north and **Dhaalu** in the south. Southern Nilandhoo is where the two vacation resorts are—both of them are located in the northeastern reef zone which affords them good protection all year round. There is only one resort on much smaller Faafu to the north. Both atolls have many small fishing villages on them and Rinbudhoo in the northwest lagoon of Dhaalu is famous for the jewelry made by the locals. Steeped in history, the islands came into the public eye when the Norwegian adventurer Thor Heyerdahl (of Kon-Tiki fame) performed extensive excavations on them and discovered seven ancient Hindu temples. Filitheyo in the north has a great house reef and is perfect for exploring either on scuba or by snorkeling as there is very little current. It has a super range of colorful soft and hard corals. Critter hunting is common here and there are several species of shrimp, nudibranch, and clownfish to see. With only a few resorts around Nilandhoo, the dive sites are much quieter and, more often than not, you will find yourself on reefs that remain relatively unexplored.

ABOVE: Divers often swim over a reef without pausing to notice the wealth of colorful marine life, such as giant anemones and clownfish, that lies there in such abundance.
OPPOSITE: Many divers come to the Maldives to experience close-up encounters with giant manta rays which come to the cleaning stations to be rid of their parasites.

"... it is the mantas that everyone comes for, although sightings are not guaranteed ..."

Fact file Maldives

BEST TIME TO GO
There are two distinct seasons in the northeastern Indian Ocean and the current pattern changes accordingly with the monsoons. Dive conditions during the dry season are at their optimum with only light winds and currents coming from the northeast between November and April. The optimum times to visit are November to April for the west reefs and August to November for the east reefs.

UNDERWATER VISIBILITY AND TEMPERATURE
Visibility is usually in excess of 100ft (30m) on the outer reefs, but expect it to be greatly reduced on an outgoing tide, when the current picks up all the detritus and sand particles from the inner lagoons. The temperature averages 81–84°F (27–29°C) throughout the year.

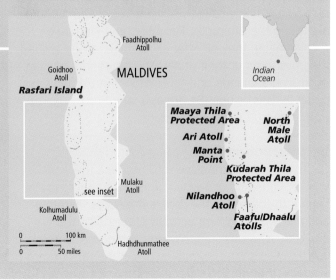

Seychelles

Indian Ocean

The Seychelles (and in particular Praslin) were hailed as the original "Garden of Eden" by General Charles Gordon (of Khartoum fame) who visited the islands in 1881 to advise on their fortification. The name alone sounds exotic and conjures up images of palm-fringed white sandy beaches, crystal clear warm waters, coral-fringed atolls, and brightly colored tropical fish. Those imagined thoughts turn to reality when you touch down on Mahé, the main island in the Seychelles archipelago, which lies just 4° south of the equator. Even though they are so close to the equator, the Seychelles enjoy a varied climate and seasons. These are marked primarily by the shift of the monsoon winds.

The Seychelles were formed at the time when Africa split away from India in the Precambrian period more than 650 million years ago. Consisting almost entirely of granite, the main islands have little or no fringing reef for protection. Indeed, some of the larger granite outcrops in Bunyore, Kenya were formed at the same time as the Seychelles group. All of the main island group in the north are granitic in origin with the exception of Dennis and Bird Islands, which are the only true coral islands. Also part of the Seychelles dominion is Aldabra, the largest coral atoll on the planet. Located midway between Mahé and Aldabra are found the Amirante, Farquhar, and Alphonse archipelagos; they all offer exceptional diving around the outer rims of their atolls. The Amirantes consist of eight single islands and three atolls with the largest being Ile Desroches. St. Joseph, and Poivre are the other two true atolls found here.

Ile Desroches

Southeast of the massive atoll reef lies the well-developed island of Ile Desroches. A trip across the lagoon to the rim of the reef is always exhilarating and many of the dives actually start inside the rim and drop down through caverns and caves, carved out over millennia. Swimming under the reef toward a speck of blue in the distance is quite a way to start the dive—you appear on the outer wall in broad daylight surrounded by brilliant red gorgonian sea fans and thousands of fish. Butteflyfish and angelfish are everywhere as are glassy sweepers, large soldierfish, various snapper, and of course the ubiquitous anemonefish and many large anemones. Protected from commercial fishing practices, diving the virgin reefs in this isolated location is unlike anything else that you may experience in the Indian Ocean.

The Northern Islands

Resembling the offshore granite islands in Thailand, the main group of the Seychelles islands in the north are not known for fantastic coral reefs as the smooth, hard rock surface leaves very little foothold for corals, sponges, or algae to adhere to. Most of the better coral growths are found inshore in shallow water of under 27ft (8m) where many of the night dives are concentrated. However, a curious hard rock shelf littered with boulder-sized granite "marbles" is found on the offshore shallow banks at depths of around 120ft (37m). The cracks and fissures in the shelf have small scrubby corals with sandy gullies and the boulders are home to various hard and soft corals. Golden cup corals, small purple rope sponges, and numerous hydroids and fire corals predominate, along with fine examples of whip corals and bubble coral. **Shark Bank** in particular is a great place to dive and exemplifies these offshore granite banks. It is home to some huge stingrays and large numbers of grey reef sharks.

What the islands lack in colorful coral, they more than make up for in species diversity. More than 900 species of fish have been recorded around the islands and several hundred types of invertebrate, making them great for critter hunting. On night dives you can find Spanish dancers (*Hexabranchus sanguineus*) and their attendant symbiotic emperor shrimp (*Periclimenes imperator*) and even the sea urchin shrimp (*Stegopontonia commensalis*), more commonly found in Indonesia. The best night dive by far is around the little rocky clump called **L'Ilot**

off the northwest coast of Mahé near Beau Vallon Bay. L'Ilot lies just a few hundred yards offshore and is separated by a channel around 70ft (22m) deep where there is a pile of overlapping small boulders. There are literally thousands of Durban hingebeak shrimp (*Rhynchocinetes durbanensis*) here, as well as small moray eels, anemones, and clownfish, tiger cowries, and small scrubby corals. The granite islet is topped with a palm tree and the sides drop steeply to around 40ft (12m) before the sand slope tapers away. Balloonfish, barracuda, snapper, and coral grouper are all common—this little clump of rocks is a real haven for a variety of marine life.

Much of the diving around Mahé is in fairly shallow water and while the reefs are not brilliant, the

ABOVE: Symbiotic emperor shrimps can be found on most Spanish dancer nudibranchs. The shrimp clean the host of parasites and in return gain protection from predators.

seemingly endless number of tropical fish more than make up for them. One of my favorite sites is Whale Rocks: these huge granite blocks have a unique white gorgonian sea fan and what can only be described as "fields" of huge plate anemones each with their symbiotic partners—skunk clownfish. In fact three species of clownfish are found here, as well as large stingrays, pincushion starfish, and numerous shells. Horseshoe Rocks is another favorite dive where moray eels can be found as well as the rare black lionfish.

Nudibranchs are also common here, as are large schools of jacks and barracuda.

The Seychelles are also special because they are on the migration route of the largest fish in the sea, the whale shark. Whale sharks (*Rhincodon typus*) follow a two-year migratory pattern that takes them all around the Indian Ocean. Often the first sightings of these massive sharks are made south of Mozambique in April and May. They then continue into the Indian Ocean and up to the Seychelles group where they congregate around the St. Anne Marine National Park from August through to November. You may be lucky enough to dive with a dozen or more of these huge fish on just one dive. When you are in the water with very poor visibility due to the plankton bloom, it can be quite disconcerting when a massive mouth suddenly appears in front of you, gulping down millions of gallons of water and filtering out the plankton as it feeds.

Reefs and wrecks

Inshore off **Beau Vallon Bay** are several small reefs and a few wrecks. The Barges, found at 90ft (25m), consists of two 66ft (20m) steel barges that were deliberately sunk in deep waters to form an artificial reef and complement a superb natural coral reef in the shallows. Although they are fairly well encrusted, the visibility is limited, but it pays to get in close for the chance to see millions of glassy sweepers and even harlequin shrimp. Nearby **Corsair Reef** is covered with soft corals and anemones, while whitetip reef sharks cruise the edge between the reef and the Barges. The Barges also play host to lobster, large schools of striped catfish, and many species of snapper and angelfish.

The largest wreck in Seychelles waters is the ***Ennerdale*** which is found about an hour's boat trip away from Mahé on a shallow bank where the ship ran aground in 1970. Striking a submerged reef, she quickly rolled over and sank, unfortunately releasing oil into the water. This was cleaned up quickly before any environmental damage could occur and the ship is now well broken up. The water column is home to hundreds of large batfish which may follow you on the entire dive. Visibility is not great at around 60ft (18m).

The ship can be negotiated on one dive, but at 100ft (30m) deep you have limited time, so it is better to visit over several dives so that you have time to get into the shaded areas to see the moray eels and stingrays. The crumpled bows tend to attract a congregation of stingrays and small whitetip reef sharks, but these soon head off into the blue as you approach them. The tangled superstructure is interesting and, as it is quite open, it allows for relatively safe exploration. Due to the depth limitations of the wreck, it is sensible to swim back toward the stern where numerous moray eels, schools of batfish, and golden snapper will vie for your attention. From here there is a safe and easy access up the mooring line to the awaiting dive boat.

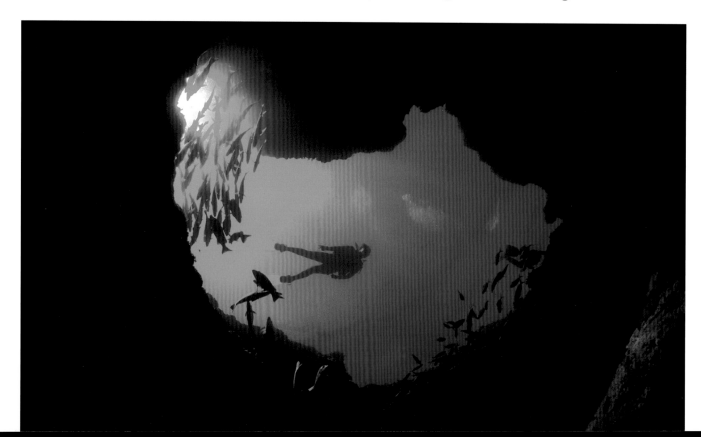

OPPOSITE: The circular caverns of Ile Desroches are very distinctive. This is a great way to start a dive to the outer reef.

ABOVE: Large numbers of whale sharks congregate at the St. Anne Marine National Park to feed on the rich plankton.

Fact file Seychelles

BEST TIME TO GO

The southeast monsoon blows from April to October; this is usually warm and dry and pushes a nutrient-rich current through the islands. Whale shark season is normally from August to late October or early November, when the heaviest rain arrives. The islands are incredibly green and tropical in appearance, so you can expect rain almost any time.

UNDERWATER VISIBILITY AND TEMPERATURE

The visibility is never particularly good as all the reefs are quite shallow and surrounded by sandy areas; it averages around 80ft (25m). Water temperature averages 82°F (28°C) in summer, and 79°F (26°C) in winter.

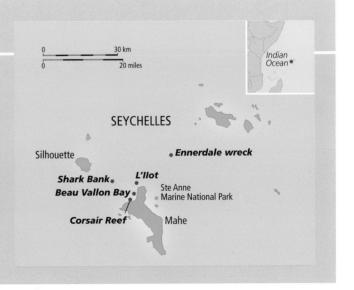

South Africa

South Atlantic/Indian Ocean

For many people South Africa conjures up visions of wildlife safaris, diamonds, Table Mountain, and Nelson Mandela. Diving does not necessarily enter this equation, but when you consider that the cool Agulhas current that flows up the east coast of South Africa brings with it probably the largest concentrations of fish and predator species ever found in one area, it certainly should.

Other attractions include the most southerly coral reefs in the world at Sodwana Bay near the border with Mozambique, numerous offshore fossilized reef beds around Aliwal Shoal, and the **Protea Banks**, and diving with great white sharks. It all adds up to a marine wonderland that will suit all tastes and levels of expertise.

Sardine run

During June and July each year millions of sardines —actually the Southern African pilchard (*Sardinops sagax*)—follow a tail of the cold water Agulhas current below 68°F (20°C) up the coast after they have spawned in the current which will eventually sweep east after it reaches Mozambique. This marine migration is vital as a food source not only for the local human population, but also for 15,000 or so common dolphins, 180,000 Cape gannets, as well as countless cetaceans including pantropical dolphins,

bottlenose dolphins, humpback whales, Bryde's whales, pilot whales, and the occasional orca. Of course, sharks are also attracted to this massive movement of fish and these predators include bronze whalers, tiger sharks, blacktip sharks, ragged-tooth sharks, dusky sharks, and Zambezi (bull) sharks. Even African black penguins and Cape fur seals join in this game of life and death.

Unfortunately the timing of the sardine run relies entirely on the current, and the fish. One good friend of mine wasted over $10,000 sitting around on a boat for two weeks vainly waiting for the action to start. It is always better to make other plans while in South Africa to take advantage of some of the more accessible diving available if the run doesn't begin on schedule. Little is known about the sardine run phenomenon, except that the water temperature has to dip below 70°F (21°C) in order for the migration to take place.

Aliwal Shoal, an ancient fossilized sand dune, is named after a three-masted ship called the *Aliwal* that just avoided sinking here back in 1849. This same shallow reef was responsible for the sinking of the *Nebo* in 1884 and the *Produce* in 1974. Access to Aliwal Shoal and the shipwrecks is possible through the several diving centers that operate from the town of Umkomaas, where their inflatables jostle amid the waves and sand banks at the mouth of the Umkomaas River. These boat handlers are incredibly skillful, racing along the wave troughs, then jumping the wave to land in the next trough, and so on, until they reach open water to make the half-hour run out to the shoal. It's exhilarating to say the least. The shallow rocky reef is home to many species of soft and hard corals, colorful sponges, and (unexpectedly) a huge number of more tropical Indian Ocean species of fish and invertebrates.

The shoal is 3 miles (5km) offshore and consists of a curious mix of ridges, sculpted caverns, underhanging ledges, and low uniform banks. All of these are topped with small sea fans, colorful sponges, and algae. Turtles are common as are

regular sightings of common dolphins. Tropical fish are found in abundance, although unfortunately the visibility is usually not particularly good. At an average depth of around 60ft (18m), the low light levels can often feel like a night dive.

South Africa is also synonymous with shark diving, whether this takes the form of free-swimming with great whites, viewing them through cages while the water is being chummed with bait, or enjoying seeing sand tigers (*Carcharias taurus*) in their natural state out on Aliwal Shoal. They are also known as ragged-toothed sharks or "raggies" to the locals! These sharks look ferocious because of their forward-pointing teeth, but are actually quite placid. They are

ABOVE: The annual sardine run attracts many different cetaceans including this Bryde's whale which suddenly appeared beneath the shoal, scooping up masses of fish.
OPPOSITE: Turtles are common around the offshore reefs, often sleeping under ledges at night. They are frequently attended by various remora or suckerfish.

seen in large aquaria all over the world, and are in fact the most widely kept captive shark.

The most southerly coral reefs in the world are located about 230 miles (370km) north of Durban at **Sodwana Bay**. Part of the Maputaland Marine Reserve, this has the only scuba diving area along the Greater St. Lucia Wetlands Park coastline (now renamed iSimangaliso). Here a sandy beach, backed by the largest sand dunes in the southern hemisphere, plays host to more hair-raising antics by the local boat handlers. The reefs are uninspiringly named after the distance they are located from the shore base (i.e. 2-mile reef, 3-mile reef, etc.). On your return to the beach, the boat captains jam the throttle on full and drive the rigid-hulled boats right up onto the beach where they come to a juddering halt.

These reefs are subject to the oceanic swell and might of the Indian Ocean, so you should expect surge on most dives. The corals are low-lying but interesting and have a great mix of tropical fish

and invertebrates. Expect to see several species of moray eels, angelfish, butterflyfish, while there are always glassy sweepers, hatchetfish, and numerous parrotfish and wrasse. All the reefs are quite separate and have wide sandy plains between them with a few isolated coral heads which abound with life, including cleaning stations where both predator and prey line up to be cleaned of parasites. This is a very popular dive area with more than 35,000 visitors each year who come to delight in the 95 species of coral and more than 1,200 varieties of fish.

From Sodwana Bay, it is well worth taking a long 4x4 trek along the beach at low tide toward the Mozambique border to **Mabibi Lagoon**. Here there are massive rock pools, some over 7ft (2m) deep, where snorkeling around the rim is superb. There are many species here including lionfish, scorpionfish, wrasse, parrotfish, and many different snails and nudibranchs. At low tide, the local KwaZulu women forage along the outer shore for rock oysters and crab.

Diving with great white sharks (*Carcharodon carcharias*) is now a well established pastime around the world. This type of underwater encounter was championed off **Shark Alley** near the town of Gansbaai on the southwestern tip of South Africa. Port Lincoln in Australia and Guadaloupe Island off the coast of Mexico/California are also well known for this type of shark diving. All this sort of diving happens inside cages and the sharks are baited to come in close for the best of the action. There have been some rather unscrupulous activities carried out by some news and movie production companies to get the sharks to behave with spectacularly aggressive effect. It's done purely for the drama. We all know of this large shark's deadly reputation, but any attacks upon swimmers can hardly be blamed on the shark in the first place. To see this magnificent beast in its natural habitat is simply awesome and, while it is the bait that brings them in and the watching divers are penned in cages, the effect is still fantastic. At around 20ft (6m) long and weighing over 2,200lb (1,000kg), they are powerful enough to launch their bodies clear out of the water.

These sharks can sense the blood enzyme in the water from over 1,100yd (1km) away and not long after the water is baited for the show at Shark Alley the first sharks appear. Their principal diet is Cape fur seals and large numbers of them live around the kelp forests of Geyser and Dyer Islands. The great whites clearly have an easy and almost unlimited food source, which makes the cage encounters relatively easy and untroubled. Situated just a couple of hours drive east of Cape Town, trips normally start at around 10 a.m. with transfers to Kleinbaai, just along the coast from the fishing village of Gansbaai. It is a 5-mile (8-km) trip out to Dyer Island. Undoubtedly these encounters are artificially staged, but nevertheless the experience is superb. Shark cage diving is definitely here to stay.

OPPOSITE: Diving with great white sharks is a spectator sport where divers stay in shark cages for safety, while the water is chummed all around them for some real "in-your-face" encounters with one of the world's apex predators.

Fact file South Africa

BEST TIME TO GO
June and July for the sardine run and August to November for the raggies on Aliwal Shoal. High season for the great whites is April to October, but sharks are usually seen all year round at Shark Alley—they are just so used to getting fed!

UNDERWATER VISIBILITY AND TEMPERATURE
Visibility is extremely variable and usually averages around 20–30ft (6–9m), but can stretch to around 50ft (15m) inshore. You can expect better visibility offshore if you fancy the sardine run. Sea temperature averages between 63–72°F (17–22°C) in the north and is fairly stable at around 59°F (15°C) in the south.

NAMIBIA
BOTSWANA
SWAZILAND
Mabibi Lagoon
Sodwana Bay
LESOTHO
Durban
Aliwal Shoal
SOUTH AFRICA
Protea Banks
Cape Town
Port Elizabeth
Gansbaai Shark Alley
500 km
300 miles
Indian Ocean

Malaysia

Indo-Pacific

A sprawling archipelago of many thousands of islands lying between the Indian and Pacific Oceans, Malaysia is a confederation of 13 states and three federal territories. This vast country consists of two parts: Peninsular (or West) Malaysia is located to the south of Thailand on the Malay Peninsula while East Malaya or Malaysian Borneo comprises the territories of Sarawak and Sabah on the island of Borneo. Species diversity is at its peak here where the calmer waters of the Indian Ocean meet the stronger-moving waters of the South China Sea.

What strikes the traveler most is how safe the country is to travel around. Tourists from all over the world come to visit the pristine beaches, the many national parks and reserves, the famous orangutan sanctuary at Sandakan, and of course, to enjoy the crystal-clear waters and superb coral reefs. Over one million years ago this region was undergoing tremendous volcanic activity.

The majestic mountain range of Semporna was formed as well as the Sulu archipelago. Much of the undeveloped areas of the country are covered in tropical rainforest while below the water there are superb coral reefs, majestic walls, and huge numbers of species of fish and invertebrates. Malaysia still gets its fare share of Indian Ocean species, but the country is also bathed by the waters of the South China Sea. It is near the hub of world's marine life diversity so you can expect to see a huge variety of species on every dive. Brilliantly colored soft corals and huge sponges vie for space amid sea fans, precious black corals, and a myriad brilliantly colored tropical fish and invertebrates.

Peninsular Malaysia

The more northerly islands of Peninsular Malaysia and their fringing reefs are very reminiscent of Thailand and are not as interesting as those in the south. It is only when you get to the offshore resorts that the diving action gets better. Most of the diving in Malaysia takes place around the many offshore island resorts with the Perhentian Islands and Pulau Redang

in the **Terengganu Marine Park** to the east and Pulau Tioman to the south perhaps being the most popular. All the diving around these islands is fairly shallow and visibility may be reduced with maximum depths at around 100ft (30m). The steeply sloping reefs are well encrusted with leathery corals, small soft corals, and whip corals. Some of the boulder slopes have small caverns where sharks, moray eels, and rays are common. The offshore islands are also home to large numbers of schooling fusiliers, and you can expect to see turtles on most dives as there are nesting beaches within the marine reserve.

Pulau Tioman is located in the Seri Buat archipelago and many of the 64 or so islands here have steeply sloping sides. Their southerly location yields common sightings of manta rays and whale sharks as the currents that pass through the Malacca Straits push masses of water up the east coast of Peninsular Malaysia between Borneo, Singapore, and Sumatra in Indonesia. Divers can expect to find large concentrations of angelfish and butterflyfish as well as millions of chromis, damselfish, humbug fish, and at least four or five species of clownfish and their host anemones. The deeper walls all have large pale gorgonian sea fans, some of which are over 7ft (2m) tall. If you look closely at these, you should find axilspot hogfish and longnosed hawkfish—they love this type of environment.

East Malaya

Over off the northwest coast of Borneo is **Layang-Layang** which is one of only a handful of true coral atolls which have formed over millennia with the rising waters. They are located among the Spratly Islands, the ownership of which is still contested by Malaysia's neighbors. There are hundreds of islands and seamounts in this region. Layang-Layang is one of the largest and has precipitous reef walls plummeting

OPPOSITE: Fantastically shaped soft and hard corals, surrounded by millions of colorful fish, are the essence of diving in these abundantly populated waters.

hundreds of feet into the South China Sea. Virtually all of the diving here is drift diving and there are regular sightings of large pelagics such as manta rays and hammerhead sharks. The coral reefs are spectacular and you will find "hanging gardens" of small primrose-yellow soft corals, huge forests of gorgonian sea fans, and meadows of garden eels in the sheltered sandy lagoon. Eagle rays and stingrays are common and the variety of tropical fish that will be encountered here is fantastic.

The northern region of Borneo is known as Sabah. Off the northeastern coast and abutting the border with the Indonesian province of Kalimantan are the two coral islands of Mabul and Kapalai, and Malaysia's only oceanic island of Pulau Sipadan. All Malaysia's islands lie on the continental shelf and have depths averaging only 330ft (100m). Between the edge of the continental shelf and Sipadan lies a trough 3,300ft (1,000m) deep. The living reef that we are privileged to see only accounts for the top 165ft (50m) or so, but its profile and other characteristics are influenced by the deep and precipitous nature of the island. The terrain that you see is only the tip of a submarine volcano which rises from the seabed some 2,000–2,300ft (600–700m) down on the northern margin of the Celebes Sea.

There is one particular dive which provides a poignant reminder of the fragility of all marine life. In the caves there is a narrow side passage that opens up into a second cavern, known locally as the **Turtle Tomb**. Originally discovered by Jacques Yves Cousteau, it was first thought to be the marine equivalent of the elephant's last resting place. The truth is much less romantic. Turtles sleep underwater and you can see them on ledges all around this coral island. What actually happened was that turtles swam into the cavern system to look for a safe place to sleep away from predators. Subsequently, they were unable to find their way out and drowned.

The Turtle Tomb is both awesome and humbling. The floor of the cavern is littered with skeletons, with many more lying underneath the fine silt. The remains are soon picked clean by the thousands of shrimp, transparent crabs, and numerous large worms which inhabit the cave. There are also a number of predatory fish that hunt in this eerie darkness. One of the skeletons was clearly a female because the remains of her leathery eggs are still visible.

Mabul

Pulau Sipadan was once *the* place for discerning divers but it is no longer open to tourists wanting to stay on the island. However, the island is still visited daily by dive boats from nearby Mabul and Kapali. The diving is still excellent and divers can expect to see turtles on every dive. The walls and reefs are still very good, although the visibility is variable and not as clear as one would expect from an offshore island.

Mabul is where most divers stay and it has become quite famous for its "muck diving." Mabul offers a pretty good selection of marine life and you will encounter weird frogfish, mushroom coral pipefish, curious scorpionfish, harlequin shrimp, cuttlefish, various types of spider crab, octopus, and anemonefish. Visibility is rather poor and the reef isn't that great, but for those divers who love scrabbling about on the seabed looking for interesting critters, Mabul is worth exploring while you are also diving the better reefs of Sipadan.

Pulau Kapalai

The island of **Pulau Kapalai** is actually a giant sandbar and it has one resort with 40 chalets perched on stilts in the lagoon. **Kapalai** is more a place to stay than a dive destination, but many guests at the resort think that the shallow diving is excellent too, and it saves the long boat ride to Sipadan. The coral generates much of the food needed to sustain the vast array of creatures which make up this fragile ecosystem. Sponges and brightly colored sea squirts grow amid the coral trees and everywhere are seen crawling, slithering shells, sea slugs, crabs, shrimp, starfish, and other citizens of the reef. Standing guard in caves or cruising around the steep slopes, an ever-moving blanket of fish stretches everywhere. Angels and butterflies, sweetlips and clowns, parrots and lions, sweepers and eels all live in, around and over the reef. Tiny squadrons flit among the coral branches, while others live in symbiosis with anemones, sea urchins, and feather stars.

OPPOSITE: The false clown anemonefish (*Amphiprion ocellaris*) is commonly found on its host anemone and often large numbers of them are found together in the same locality.

ABOVE: The near vertical walls are covered with soft corals and colorful anthias. Schools of fusiliers and jacks are a constant backdrop to these dives.

Fact file Malaysia

BEST TIME TO GO
The prevailing winds blow from the southwest from May to September and from the northeast from November to March. Assuming you are staying on one of the islands, you will be able to find a lee shore. There are no real seasons for seeing the large creatures, as they appear sporadically. Turtles are seen all year round, but a number of the resorts close during the monsoon season of November to March.

UNDERWATER VISIBILITY AND TEMPERATURE
Visibility averages around 60–80ft (18–25m), but can easily be over 100ft (30m) around Layang-Layang and Sipadan. The water temperature varies little between 75–82°F (24–28°C) and full wet suits are recommended.

Western Indonesia

Indo-Pacific

Indonesia is by far the largest island nation on the planet; it comprises over 17,000 islands, coral cays, and atolls. It spans almost 3,000 miles (5,000km) of ocean from the northwest tip of Sumatra to the lofty peaks of West Papua in the east. These peaks are snowcapped for most of the year, while other parts of Indonesia, like Nusa Tengarra, have an almost arid landscape reminiscent of Malta and Gozo in the Mediterranean. Other islands are lush and tropical and filled with with exotic sounds and the cries of monkeys permeating through the jungle.

Around 250 million people live in the country and they encompass hugely diverse political and religious backgrounds. Muslim Arab traders were the first to visit the islands from the seventh century onward, but the more northerly islands are now predominantly Christian. Buddhism and Hinduism are also strong, particularly in Bali, while Dutch, German, Portuguese, and Chinese traders have all influenced this amazing melting pot of a nation.

Huge rivers traverse the region, and while many islands support thriving industries or have a significant agricultural output, others are deserted. All of them, without fail, maintain the most diverse and amazing marine habitats—more species of marine life are found here than at any other place on the planet. Diving areas such as Manado in northern Sulawesi near the Bunaken National Marine Park support more fish on their house reef than anywhere else; the Raja Ampat archipelago in the far eastern province of West Papua has more species recorded than any other single site in the world. Now multiply that by the 17,000 or so islands and you reach mind-boggling statistics. Considering that only a handful of these islands are properly explored, it is obvious that the future for diving here is boundless.

Virtually all of the diving is done by boat. Many only require a short ride to the nearby reefs, while a number of live-aboard dive boats also ply these waters. Depending on the season, they will take the long run through the middle of the island chain, always looking for new and exciting areas to dive.

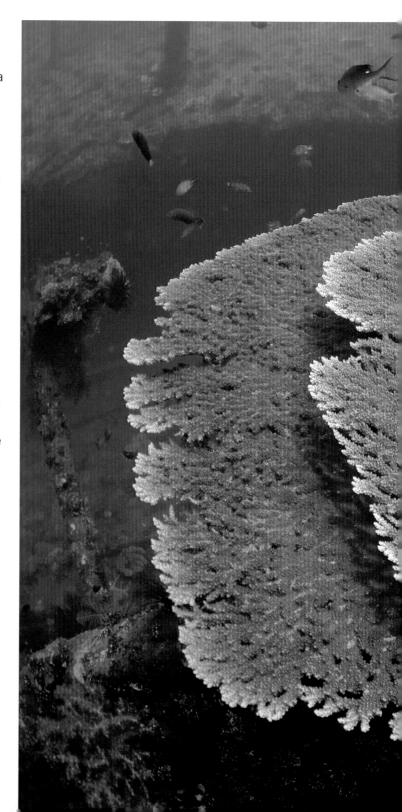

LEFT: Beautifully camouflaged Coleman's shrimp make their home amidst the spines of a poisonous sea urchin, snipping off spines to make their position more comfortable.
BELOW: Large table corals and crinoids stretch out into the current from one of the best shipwrecks in the world, the *Liberty*, which lies off the coast of Bali.

All the diving resorts have their house reefs and you can shore dive to your heart's content, particularly at night when a myriad other creatures—unseen during the day—come out to play. Visibility is generally very good except in the Lembeh Straits, which is now the generally acclaimed "muck-diving capital of the world." Each dive here is like a night dive at the edge of a huge commercial fishing lane, but the number of critters to be found here is incredible.

Coral reefs

Indonesia is home to around 15% of the world's coral reefs lying along the 50,000 miles (80,000km) of coastline. There is probably twice that number in total if you also take into account all of the patch reefs, isolated atolls and coral heads, marine mountains, and hidden shoals. More than 4,000 species of fish are found here, compared to the mere 400 species in the Caribbean. Invertebrates are countless and large numbers of cetaceans also make these waters home. Dugong are found, as are sea snakes and turtles. There are also lots of shipwrecks which have come to grief on these shallow reefs.

Pulau Sangalaki

The western region of Indonesia off the shore of Kalimantan has a small number of well-established resorts, all of which are famous for their marine life and diverse habitats. It is a bit like "trial by ordeal" to get to **Pulau Sangalaki** off the east coast of Kalimantan as it involves either a one-hour flight from Tawau or Balikpapan to Berau, followed by a two-hour boat journey down the scenic Berau River, before crossing over the shallow lagoon to the island. This protected marine sanctuary is surrounded by shallow reefs, some of which lie in almost concentric circles with a wide sandy area between. The lagoon is a natural hatchery for many species of fish and it takes 10 to 20 minutes by boat to get out to the dive sites as the inner lagoon is so shallow. However, when you do reach the reefs, they are all under 65ft (20m) and in pristine condition.

There are more than 500 species of coral recorded here and all of them are thronging with a dazzling mixture of shoaling fusiliers, trevally, chromis, unicornfish, batfish, and surgeonfish.

RIGHT: Huge gorgonian sea fans stretch out into the prevailing currents and these in turn are host to a remarkable collection of different fish and invertebrates.

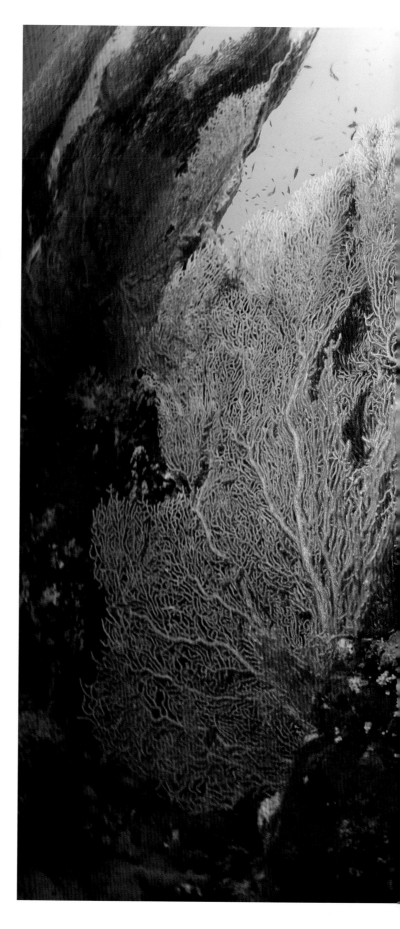

Among the corals are humbugfish, at least six species of anemonefish, cardinalfish, countless types of damselfish, wrasse, and squirrelfish. Happily the larger predators are also present here including whitetip reef sharks. Mantas and eagle rays frequent the lagoon area as well as crocodilefish, garden eels, and lots of blennies and gobies. It is the manta rays that particularly attract divers to Sangalaki as more than 50 of these massive, graceful rays can be seen in huge feeding formations around the island. Hundreds of species of nudibranch are found in all of the habitats, which makes it a photographer's dream, and amazingly colored shrimp are seen everywhere.

While there is plenty in the immediate area of Sangalaki to satisfy most people's diving or underwater photographic needs, the resort also offers day trips to the neighboring islands of Pulau Derawan, Pulau Samama, Pulau Kakaban, and Pulau Maratua. Virtually all of the diving is either in or around the shallow lagoons or drift diving from the day dive boats at the entrances to the lagoon channels.

Pulau Derawan

Located in a biodiversity hotspot, **Pulau Derawan** is rapidly gaining popularity with critter hunters, particularly around the pilings of the 600ft- (180m-) long jetty. There is an absolutely amazing array of small marine organisms and it easily rivals Lembeh, the muck diving capital of the world. There are dwarf scorpionfish, pufferfish, sea cucumbers, tiny juvenile frogfish, sea horses, cleaner shrimp, banded shrimp, cuttlefish, dragonets, banded pipefish, mantis shrimp, thousands of shrimp gobies, and the attendant shrimp which make their burrows. All divers can expect to see both green and hawksbill turtles on every dive as there are nesting sites for both species on Derawan. Over 50 species of *Acropora* coral have been recorded on one reef here and species diversity is abundant as the island has a wide range of habitats with sloping reefs, vertical walls, sheltered lagoons, a pier, and numerous caverns. Visibility is not normally as good here as on the outer islands, but it doesn't really matter when you are working so close to the edge of the reef or seabed looking for some of the most weird and wonderful species of marine life in the ocean.

OPPOSITE: The large caves and caverns support huge schools of red soldierfish that are always near the entrances and make a great addition to underwater photographs.

BELOW: The black-saddled toby (*Canthigaster valentini*) is a type of pufferfish that forms mating pairs for life. They can be seen flitting around the coral heads looking for small crustaceans and invertebrates to eat.

Fact file Western Indonesia

BEST TIME TO GO
February to August are considered the best for access to the reefs and the best of the sea conditions.

UNDERWATER VISIBILITY AND TEMPERATURE
Visibility on the offshore reefs is always over 100ft (30m), although it can be reduced to around 40–50ft (12–15m) where the islands are surrounded by sandy plains which reduces the visibility exponentially. Averages 82°F (28°C) in summer and only dropping to 79°F (26°C) in winter.

Pulau Kakaban

Covered with dense jungle right down to the water's edge, the island of **Pulau Kakaban** surprisingly also has a jellyfish lake similar to that found in Palau in the western Pacific. At 2sq miles (5km^2) this mangrove-fringed lake is grand in scale and presents a spectacle that is a constant reminder of how species can adapt in isolation in different parts of the world. The reefs around Kakaban are also very colorful and the northern point usually has large numbers of jacks, barracuda, and manta rays which tend to congregate at the entrance into the inner lagoon. Further east still is the huge atoll of Nabucco with Pulau Maratua to the north and the more isolated islet of Bakungan in the south. This large horseshoe-shaped coral island has numerous turtle nesting beaches and the locals swear that this is the turtle center for all of Indonesia. Diving is still relatively new here, but gratifyingly there is a very wide variety on offer to dive tourists here as well as at other nearby islands.

Pulau Maratua

Maratua has a variety of dives along steeply sloping walls and coral rubble on the resort's house reef where mandarinfish are found each evening as the sun goes down. Stargazers, ornate ghost pipefish, cuttlefish, and tiny octopuses are found here as well as a huge variety of shrimp and crabs that come out to forage each night. Large basket starfish, crinoids, and sea urchins all have their symbiotic house guests and there are nudibranchs by the score. Off the points where the current is strongest, you will encounter plenty of turtles, great shoals of trevally, amberjacks, tuna, and barracuda.

Bali

The island of Bali in the south is the epitome of an exotic location, with a fabulous culture, amazing temples, very friendly people, and perhaps the best shore diveable wreck that you can dive anywhere on Earth. Known as the **Liberty Wreck**, this US Army transport ship was launched in 1918 and was named the *Liberty*. Torpedoed during the Second World War,

BELOW AND OPPOSITE: The *Liberty* wreck off Tulamben in northeast Bali is rated as one of the top shore dives on the planet. Shipwrecks quickly become an extension of the natural reef and are soon completely festooned with coral and sponge growth, and colonized by invertebrates while the surrounding water teems with fish.

she ended up beached on the northern shore of Bali at Tulamben where she languished until 1963 until Mount Agung blew its top. The resulting ash and lava flow broke the *Liberty*'s back and pushed her over into around 120ft (36m) of water. The shoreline is now filled in with ash and little lava bombs, making shore entry quite difficult, especially if there is any swell on the water.

The seabed looks quite drab and uninteresting until you come across a straight line (which is the port side of the ship's hull). From here the entire shipwreck just spreads out below you. The hull is completely open with her holds exposed while all her ribs and superstructure, aft gun, propeller, and rudder are covered in soft and hard corals. Just off the ship in open water is an ever-present swirling mass of jacks. The water column is filled with sergeant majors and chromis, and unicornfish and surgeonfish vie for your attention. You just cannot help but swim off the wreck into the midst of the jacks to enjoy the spectacle of them swimming all around you. Toward the bow of the ship and in around 100ft (30m) are several small pink sea fans, home to pygmy sea horses (*Hippocampus bargibanti*) and solitary, large barracuda patrol the

inner recesses. This is a superb shipwreck and the chance to dive here should definitely not be missed.

The Tulamben coastline to the east of the wreck is also composed of black ash sand and slopes steeply over small boulders. Rather uninspiring at first glance, the seabed is home to an incredible array of sea urchins with Coleman's shrimp on them, harlequin shrimp, strange little snails, dozens of species of nudibranchs, and lots else in between.

Among the islands of southern Indonesia, **Nusa Penida**, between Bali and Lombok, has a cleaning station for manta rays along its south shore. The massive limestone cliffs and cool waters are very reminiscent of Gozo in the Maltese islands, but here the similarity ends, as large numbers of mantas come in to be cleaned of parasites by small angelfish and wrasse. The Gili Islands off the northwest point of Lombok are also superb, but are more suited for drift diving. There are always plenty of turtles on each dive and divers can also expect to come across pygmy sea horses, giant frogfish, sea snakes, and lots of tropical fish. The turtle sanctuary here plays a very important part in the reef ecology, particularly when there are so many tourists visiting the area.

Eastern Indonesia

Indo-Pacific

Traveling east across Indonesia into northern Sulawesi, the Bunaken Marine Park surrounds a small group of five volcanic islands which are geographically separated from the mainland by an oceanic trench that plunges 4,600ft (1,400m) deep. Deeper cold water upwellings bring a rich planktonic soup which feeds the denizens of the marine park and creates a diversity that has gained international recognition. **Bunaken** is the largest of the islands and has a huge south-facing bay that protects many fragile coral formations. On either side of the bay are Mandolin to the west and Lekuan to the east, each of which is situated at the start of amazing, vertical, precipitous walls that drop into the depths. The flat reef top between the wall and the island is reminiscent of that found at Ras Muhammad in the Red Sea and is incredibly popular with snorkelers. As always on these exposed walls, the gorgonian sea fans and whips are prolific, but they are also home to many interesting species of marine life such as blennies, shrimp, and crabs. Out in the blue you regularly see dolphins, giant grouper, huge jacks, tuna, and snapper. Sea snakes are also common and although incredibly venomous, they rarely come close to divers so do not pose a serious threat.

Off the northeast coast of Manado Tua to the west of Bunaken is **Panguilingan**. The wall starts much deeper here at over 100ft (30m) and most divers tend to spend their time on the steeply sloping reef above. There are huge examples of, well … just about everything, from table corals to barrel sponges to plate sponges, sea fans, and brain corals. Large schools of fish are always around this point, yet the smaller fish and invertebrates are also constantly vying for your attention.

Islands near Manado

Off the northern coast of Sulawesi are a number of small islands with **Gangga Island** being favored by many as a hub for exploring the area. **Bangka Island** is popular with divers as the terrain is completely different to the easier coral reefs around the shore.

Here, rocky pinnacles stretch out in the current and create impressive caverns and canyons with whip corals and colorful gorgonians deeper down that filter feed on the passing plankton. There is usually a current around the pinnacles which, at first glance, look fairly boring as you approach them down the shot line. However the main pinnacle is cut by two huge caves which connect in the center with a smaller cavern leading off to one side. The walls are covered with whip corals and gorgonians, and schools of brilliant red soldierfish are everywhere. Angelfish, butterflyfish, and pelagic jacks all congregate at this impressive site.

Nearby **Lihaga** is used for dusk diving for mandarinfish (*Synchiropus splendidus*) and this inevitably turns into a night dive after the sun has set. With patience and timing, you may be able to witness a number of different pairs of mandarinfish enjoying their courtship rituals. These spectacularly colored little fish carry out this mating ritual every night and the same routine is displayed everywhere they are found. The male performs an elaborate jerky kind of "dance" midwater to attract several females into the display area. Once the male has his sights on a particular mate, both fish come together and spiral slowly upward above the reef releasing a cloud of eggs and sperm. The performance is repeated over 45 minutes or so.

Dusk is a curiously quiet time as the daytime creatures have hidden away, and the nighttime animals and fish haven't yet ventured far into the open. With patience you should be rewarded with great photographs of the mating mandarinfish, as well as the usual shrimp and reef crabs, which start to clean the sleeping parrotfish, wrasse, and damselfish. Moray eels and blue ribbon eels (*Rhinomuraena quaesita*) are common and there are always a few small schools of fusiliers darting among the coral heads. Divers also venture from Gangga over to Bunaken in the west as well as to a number of sites along the northern shore of Sulawesi and down to the Lembeh Straits in the southeast.

Lembeh

The island of **Lembeh** is undoubtedly on everyone's diving list but surprisingly it is probably the least attractive of the diving zones as it sits along the edge of a commercial shipping lane where years of garbage have been thrown overboard. The trash has become colonized by some of the weirdest underwater critters to be found anywhere. There are two distinct zones in the Straits, the mainland to the west is volcanic and the shores have dark brown volcanic ash in place of sand. On the eastern side of the channel, the shores of Lembeh Island are of coral origin with fine white sand. The diving here is very good and also features a fair representation of weird and wonderful fish and invertebrates. The corals are in good order and while the visibility is still relatively poor, there is a good amount of light due to the reflective qualities of the white sand. Large patches of small circular mushroom corals are found here, as well as many large anemones, some of which will have at least three species of anemonefish and several types of shrimp

ABOVE: Mandarinfish are actually a species of dragonet and are only ever seen at dusk in areas of broken coral where the nightly mating ritual takes place.

and crabs. However, it is the dark shore and trash-littered seabed which is the main focus for divers.

By swimming slowly and paying attention to what is around you, you stand a good chance of seeing flamboyant cuttlefish, leafy scorpionfish, devil scorpionfish, Indian walkers, frogfish, pygmy sea horses, mimic octopuses, dwarf lionfish, nudibranchs too numerous to mention, as well as shrimp, crabs, and other weird creatures. On the shallow dark sand slope are huge anemones with various clownfish and damselfish, cleaner shrimp, and crabs in attendance. Amid all of the trash, balloonfish hide from view, their huge eyes developed for the low-light conditions in the straits. Curious relatives of scorpionfish and lionfish called *Rhinopias*—looking like Disneyesque caricatures—are also found.

Flores Island further to the south has always rated highly with divers for its fabulous walls and very colorful reefs. The island is very big, and diving tends to be concentrated in the eastern and western regions amid the jumble of small islands and rocks just offshore in each location. Small lobsters are usually to be seen, as are juvenile reef squid, which hunt in the flat reef top in the shallows.

On the outer islands in the east, Pomana Besar and Pomana Kecil both have vertical walls with a huge range of both hard and soft corals. This region has been hit by earthquakes and tidal waves in the past and while the evidence of tidal waves is long gone, you can still see cracks in the larger stony corals where the earthquake hit. There are huge Napoleon wrasse, blacktip and whitetip reef sharks, jacks, barracuda, and big schools of rainbow runners and trevallies. The reef wall is mostly hard corals, yet is covered in colorful soft corals creating thousands of crevices in which shy creatures may hide. There are friendly spotted grouper, large moray eels, and more basslets that you can shake a snorkel at!

Komodo has some outstanding drift diving, but these dives are only done by live-aboard boat that will also take in much of the Banda Sea and will certainly include Ambon in any excursion. Lembeh is always promoted for muck diving, but Ambon is also attractive because it is very uncrowded and has a vast array of frogfish, three species of pygmy sea horse, several species of ghost pipefish, weird scorpionfish, *Rhinopias*, blue ribbon eels, barramundi cod, colorful sea squirts, and many different kinds of anemonefish, octopus, squid, shrimp, and crabs.

West Papua

Traveling as far east as you can go in Indonesia you arrive in West Papua (formerly known as West Irian Jaya), part of the huge island of New Guinea. Another province of Indonesia called Papua (formerly known as Irian Jaya) lies to the east, while (confusingly) Papua New Guinea to the east is a completely separate country. The most westerly point of West Papua is where the Bird's Head Peninsula is located, as well as the Four Kings Islands, known the world over as **Raja Ampat**. Looking remarkably like the island nation of Palau from the air with tiny jungle-topped rocks surrounded by crystal clear waters, the larger islands have precipitous cliffs dropping down to a narrow band of fringing reef that plummets into the depths.

Interestingly, the coral reefs and their associated marine life are in an area with quite a high surface water temperature, suggesting that they are much less susceptible to coral bleaching than other coral areas of the world. Consequently, Raja Ampat is one of the primary sources of coral larvae and invertebrate larval dispersal throughout the "Coral Triangle," making it of utmost importance that this significant habitat should have full marine protection.

Misool, one of the larger islands, has a superb eco-resort which boasts a 470sq mile (1,220km^2) no-take zone, which includes both turtle and manta ray sanctuaries. The house reef from the resort is just a short step away along the jetty and it has been scientifically determined that there are more species of marine life here than at any other place Earth.

On the western side of Waigeo Island is **Sel Pele Bay**, the favorite haunt for critter hunters who revel

---

Fact file Eastern Indonesia

BEST TIME TO GO
March to August are considered the peak months while November to April is the monsoon season when you can expect high winds and rain. However, on such lush, green islands you can expect rain at any time, and it is often torrential.

UNDERWATER VISIBILITY AND TEMPERATURE
Visibility can be expected to be over 100ft (30m), although it is lower in the western archipelagos where the islands are surrounded by sandy plains which often get stirred up. Water temperature averages 82°F (28°C) in summer and only drops to 79°F (26°C) in winter.

Pacific Ocean

Indian Ocean

Gangga Island
Bangka Island
Lihaga Island
Bunaken
Manado
North Sulawesi
Lembeh
Panguilingan
Sel Pele Bay
Waigeo
INDONESIA
Batanta Island
Raja Ampat
West Papua
Misool

Komodo
Flores
EAST TIMOR
Sumba

0   500 km
0   300 miles

in the absurdity of the shapes and marvel at the spectacle of the colors of the marine creatures that live within the limits of this small bay. One of the top dives in the bay is Dindiung Selatan, which has depths of only 50–80ft (15–25m) and a nice wall and coral slope down to a sandy seabed dotted with small corals and many different types of sea urchin, anemone, and cucumbers. Flying gurnards, plenty of nudibranchs, shrimp, scorpionfish, anemonefish, and pipefishes are found in profusion, and of course there are also large numbers of pygmy sea horses.

At the entrance of the bay is Kebung Kerang where the reef wall drops to 100–130ft (30–40m). The coral wall is exceptional with large gorgonian sea fans, angelfish, sea squirts, and anemones with many different species of clownfish, crabs, and shrimp all living together. There is a small pearl fishery located in the bay and divers often congregate around the jetty where frogfish, robust ghost pipefish, small moray eels, mantis shrimp, nudibranchs, and tiny crabs and shrimp are always found. Night dives are common here as there is so much to discover and enjoy in such a small area.

The Jet Fam group of small islands found to the west of Batanta Island has dozens of channels through the numerous limestone islands, islets, and submerged reefs. The hard corals found here are exceptional, particularly around Batu Burung or Bird

ABOVE: Curiously shaped relatives of the scorpionfish and stonefish inhabit the black coral sand of the Lembeh Straits. Their brilliant colors make them easy to spot. Their sharp dorsal spines are highly venomous.

Rocks where large schools of bream, fusiliers, and trevally swarm past you. Anthias are a predominant feature here and you will find several different species all mixed together. With an average depth of 50ft (15m) on the inner wall, you can spend lots of time exploring and adding creatures that you have never seen before to your species list. Clown triggerfish and Picasso triggerfish are a regular sighting as are sharks and rays, but it is the colors of the angelfish and butterflyfish that are the highlight of the dive.

According to the environmental organization Conservation International, the marine surveys that have been carried out over the last few years in Raja Ampat indicate that the marine life diversity in the region is unrivaled. Over 75% of all marine species are found here. Scientists have recorded more than 1,600 species of fish, 42 of which are endemic; more than 600 species of hard coral (ten times more than there are in the Caribbean), 13 type of marine mammal, five turtle species, and thousands of invertebrates, including 57 different kinds of mantis shrimp. No wonder that Raja Ampat is classed as the number one diving location in the world.

Pacific
Ocean

Pacific Islands

Pacific Ocean

It is difficult to describe adequately the vast amount of scuba diving available in the Pacific as it is so varied. Inevitably most is concentrated in regions that have the right infrastructure to be able to host visiting divers. If you want to explore off the beaten track it will get harder and more time-consuming to reach the destination of your choice. Most of us do not have the luxury of spending many weeks or months skipping between tropical islands discovering undived reefs and wrecks, some of which still contain vast amounts of treasure dating back to the 16th century. This chapter will focus on the most frequently enjoyed diving areas in places that have enviable reputations for fantastic diving among some of the most spectacular island nations in the world. The Islands of Oceania, as they are often referred to, are nearly all located within the Tropics of Cancer and Capricorn. Australia and New Zealand are for the most part outside this zone, and then, as we travel up the west coast of continental North America to Vancouver, we enter a temperate water zone.

Melanesia is the largest subregion in Oceania and includes Papua New Guinea, the Solomon Islands, the Maluku Islands, Santa Cruz Islands, New Caledonia, Vanuatu, and Fiji.

Papua New Guinea

PNG or Papua New Guinea in the western Pacific is the eastern half of New Guinea, the second largest island in the world. The other half comprises the Indonesian provinces of Papua and West Papua. PNG measures around 750 miles (1,200km) at its widest from north to south and over 1,250 miles (2,000km) from east to west. Some estimates say this amounts to more than 6,000 islands but this figure includes all coral cays and islets which break the surface. In reality the figure is nearer 600 islands of any recognizable size. Largely under its neighbor Australia's wing, it relies heavily on the sizeable expat population to run its infrastructure. Australia's northernmost point almost touches the coast south of Daru. PNG's reefs are at the northern extremities of the Coral Sea.

While diving is limited to a few small areas, there is a fantastic mix of black sand "muck" diving in **Milne Bay** at the easternmost tip of PNG, while wrecked ships and aircraft dating from the Second World War are dotted all over the seabed. Largely intact, these metal structures are now covered with all manner of coral growth and marine organisms. North of Milne Bay, off **Dobu island**, is a site called

Bubble Bath, very similar to Danglebens, Dominica, in the Caribbean where hydrothermal vents discharge bubbles all over the reef. Nearby Egum Rock is famous for its large numbers of sharks and myriad tropical fish and very healthy corals. The Louisiade Archipelago to the southeast is also well worth exploring if you can persuade your live-aboard boat captain to steer away from the regular routes.

Most of these reefs are undived so if you want to dive away from the madding crowd, then come and explore the 15,500sq miles (40,000km^2) of coral reefs here. The coastline from Milne Bay up toward Popondetta is very interesting as there are fantastic walls, reefs, and wrecks. A number of live-aboard dive boats work in this region and you will be treated to huge gorgonian sea fan forests all topped with

ABOVE: Tube worms can be found everywhere, with their protective tubes encased in hard corals. They filter feed on the ever-present plankton in the water.
OPPOSITE: Colorful ribbon eels poke their heads out of the reef. Usually quite timid, they can be approached, but with care.

crinoids, fields of garden eels, crocodilefish, frogfish, sea moths, and nudibranchs by the score. Every night dive is another adventure as you will encounter some of the rarest shrimp and octopuses and enjoy the changes as the daytime creatures sleep and the nighttime creatures appear. Off the **Salamaua Peninsula** there are superb shallow coral gardens where cuttlefish roam. North at **Madang** intense fighting during the Second World War left a number of wrecks including an intact B-25 Mitchell aircraft.

Bismarck Archipelago

To the northeast of New Guinea is the **Bismarck Archipelago**: a group of islands including New Britain, New Ireland, and New Hanover and stretching north to the Admiralty Islands. **Kimbe Bay** off New Britain is the home hunting ground for Walindi Resort and its vertical walls and coral reefs are legendary. Various whales and dolphins are regulars in the bay, but it is really the reefs and the massive schools of fish, sharks, rays, and turtles that you come to see. Some of the walls are quite deep, but in the main the average depth here is under 100ft (30m) allowing you plenty of time to explore. The shallow sandy bays have stargazers, razorfish, commensal shrimp gobies, flounders, sea cucumbers, garden eels, and hundreds of anemones, all of which have various species of clownfish, porcelain crab, or cleaner shrimp in attendance. North around New Ireland and west around New Hanover there are massive tidal movements that push plankton-rich waters past the islands, meaning that virtually every inch of substrate is inhabited by some creature or growth of coral. The species diversity is vast, but the currents at some of the exposed corners are so strong that divers have to use "reef hooks" to stay anchored in place while they watch the large schools of sharks, barracuda, batfish, jacks, and trevally swim by. The diving operations in these areas pride themselves on exploratory diving and will quite often take you to new, unexplored reefs and shoals, just to see what is there.

Solomon Islands

Immediately to the east of PNG are the Solomon Islands. Marovo lagoon in the **New Georgia Islands** in the western Solomons is where marine scientists first took a serious look at the Pacific ecosystems and the diversity of marine life to be found in the region. This massive sheltered lagoon is one of the largest on the planet and is home to some of the most diverse marine life ecosystems ever studied. Not only are there amazing and distinct habitats in this region, there are also large numbers of military artefacts as the Solomons were heavily bombed during the Second World War. The seas were famous for the aerial attacks on warships that took place around her main island of Guadalcanal. Shallow lagoons coupled with fantastic drop-offs are the norm and drift dives are often used as the channels into the lagoon have the largest concentrations of big fish and other pelagics. The Chaparoana Channel off Uepi is particularly famous for its encounters with large sharks, mantas,

ABOVE: A juvenile humphead wrasse swims with a school of jacks just off the coral wall. Sharks and grouper also congregate when there is plenty of food.

and turtles. Ghizo Island in the west is another popular hub for diving with plenty of Second World War shipwrecks and sunken aircraft to visit, as well as fantastic coral gardens and tropical fish.

Vanuatu

To the southeast of the Solomons lies the island nation of Vanuatu, home to the world famous wreck of the **SS _President Coolidge_**. She was a luxury US liner that was launched in 1931. Working as a troop carrier and munitions transport in the Second World War, the _President Coolidge_ was sunk by "friendly" US mines as

Fact file Pacific Islands

BEST TIME TO GO

The area is so vast that the climate varies significantly—in the north it may be dry while other islands are wet. All of the diving is in sheltered bays and around reefs, so there is always somewhere sheltered to dive. It is available all year round, but the best conditions are from November to March.

UNDERWATER VISIBILITY AND TEMPERATURE

Visibility is usually in excess of 80ft (25m) and the average sea temperatures vary between 77°F (25°C) in the south to 84°F (29°C) in the Bismarck Sea.

she was trying to enter harbor at Espiritu Santu, the largest island in the Vanuatu archipelago. Regarded as one of the top shipwrecks in the world, this dive is not to be taken lightly. In fact, it is almost impossible to see the whole ship on just one visit. Sadly, many of those visiting the wreck only want to see the famous statue in the stateroom of the "Lady and the Unicorn." As the ship is lying on her starboard side, you have to orient yourself at 90° to get everything in perspective—the statue lies in 120ft (35m) of water at the end of the First-Class lounge. The dive to this part of the ship is long and in deep water, so only those with the required skills will be allowed to undertake it. With a minimum depth of 60ft (18m) and a maximum depth of 200ft (60m), this ship is a demanding dive. Visibility so close to shore is always variable, but it is rarely more than 50ft (15m) making it difficult to gain any true perspective of the entirety of the wreck when you are swimming around the hull.

ABOVE: Hawkfish hide amidst the hard corals picking off small invertebrates. Their adapted fins allow them to perch on top of the reef and "hop" from place to place.

Fiji

The Republic of Fiji to the east lies on the International Date Line and is 1,300 miles (2,100km) north of New Zealand and 2,000 miles (3,200km) northeast of Australia. The archipelago consist of more than 300 islands located in 500,000sq miles (1.3 million km^2) of ocean. The larger islands of Viti Levu, Vanua Levu, Kadavu, and Taveuni are all volcanic in origin and are surrounded by low-lying coral islands which peek above a vibrant coral reef system where more than 1,000 species of fish have been recorded. There are countless little atolls everywhere as well as scenic small mountain peaks surrounded by fringing reefs.

Fiji is probably the best location in the world to observe every stage in the formation of an atoll. Her barrier reef, which runs around almost the entire Fijian archipelago, is second to none and features spectacular vertical walls undercut in many places and riven by fissures, caverns, and canyons that are stuffed full of brilliantly colored soft corals. Some of these reefs are very reminiscent of the Red Sea, except that there are many more species of exotically colored tropical fish in evidence. Anthias are often seen amid the purple soft corals, as are lionfish, red coral grouper, and various butterflyfish and angelfish. Crocodilefish, scorpionfish, and stonefish are common, as well as schools of barracuda, batfish, emperorfish, unicornfish, and surgeonfish.

Beqa Lagoon, south of Viti Levu, is very popular with photographers, as is Namena Barrier Reef which has amazing numbers of tropical fish and invertebrates. The Somosomo Strait between Vanua Levu and **Taveuni** provides some exhilarating drift diving along vertical walls that are covered in soft corals. Diving is done by boat, as there are some notoriously strong drift dives, so divers must have the usual safety equipment such as delayed surface marker buoys (SMBs) or dive flags to allow the following ship's tender to pick them up safely. Many of the dives are in the channels, as that is where the greatest variety of marine life is found. Divers will drift through the passes, while sheltering behind any coral bommies available so as to be able to stop and take in the grandeur of the walls and the marine life that lives on the move. There are thousands of miles of barrier reef and fringing reefs to explore in this enchanting archipelago.

OPPOSITE: The coral walls and reefs of Fiji are colored with fantastic pink and purple soft corals and more than 1,000 species of fish can be found around them.

"There are thousands of miles of barrier reef and fringing reefs in this enchanting archipelago."

Micronesia

Pacific Ocean

To the north of PNG is found the Federated State of Micronesia, an independent four-state island nation consisting of more than 600 islands. Yap and Chuuk (Truk) are the main focus for divers. However, if you have the time, move on to Pohnpei and Kosrae too as they are also superb. Northwest of Yap is Guam which is considered a plum US military posting—this permanent base has more than 23,000 personnel on the islands.

The diving here among the remains of Second World War ships and aircraft is always excellent and all the reefs are protected. The islands are now very popular with Japanese tourists and large numbers of Japanese divers visit annually. More unusual dives like the Blue Hole or the Crevice are known for their superclear water, but in general it is the reefs and wrecks which are the focus at Guam. The Blue Hole off Guam's Orote Peninsula starts in around 60ft (18m) and is a natural perpendicular shaft that drops to around 300ft (90m). At 130ft (40m) a window opens out to the outside wall and this is the part of the dive that everyone loves. After the freefall down the shaft, it is just great to come out into the blue amid large schools of fish.

Palau

To the southwest of Chuuk is the independent Presidential Republic of **Palau**, a nation consisting of 250 islands. Geographically within Micronesia and almost due north of Raja Ampat, Palau has entered into a Compact of Free Association with the United States of America which provides social services, funding, and defense. Once owned by Spain, Germany, and Japan, Palau came under the protection of the United States when it was taken in 1944 at dreadful cost to both US and Japanese servicemen.

When flying into the main island of Babeldaob, you will inevitably pass over the wonderfully scenic Seventy Islands Wildlife Preserve. Better than picture postcard perfect, visitors are not allowed here. The islands are a very important site for turtles, seabirds, and as a hatchery for many species of marine organism. The islands of Babeldaob, Koror, and Peleliu are connected by a fantastic barrier reef. The island of Angaur to the south is an isolated oceanic island. To the west are the incredible uninhabited **Rock Islands** and to the north can be found the coral atoll of Kayangel.

Known internationally as having some of the best wall diving in all of the Pacific, the underwater topography of Palau is simply outstanding. Some of the currents are so strong that you are advised to bring reef hooks to allow you to anchor yourself onto a piece of dead coral. Then you can just hang effortlessly in the current as you watch large schools of sharks, batfish, jacks, barracuda, and unicornfish glide by. Mantas are common on many of the exposed headlands and the channel into Ngerdmaru Bay is (almost) as famous as Miil Channel on Yap.

Not only are the reefs spectacular, there is also a heady combination of Second World War shipwrecks and downed aircraft smothered in soft and hard corals, precious black corals and some 1,800 species of fish. The most popular sites like the **Big Drop-Off** and **Blue Corner** are perfect for reef hooks. The reefs around Peleliu to the south of the archipelago are often blown out due to high winds, but sites such as Orange Beach are interesting because of the number of sunken amphibious vehicles there. Large schools of fusiliers, leopard sharks, and turtles are common too. Honeymoon Beach on the eastern side is popular for the smaller invertebrates such as harlequin shrimp (*Hymenocera elegans*).

Off the western reefs of Ngemelis are several outstanding sites with Blue Corner and the **Blue Holes** probably at the top of everyone's list. This reef juts out into the current and is principally a flat

OPPOSITE: Jellyfish Lake contains thousands of nonstinging jellyfish which move around, following the sun, causing symbiotic algae to grow in their bodies, which they feed on. There are four other lakes teeming with jellyfish in the same vicinity.

area of reef around 45ft (13m) deep that then drops steeply into the depths. The Blue Holes are not true blue holes such as are found in the Caribbean, rather these are naturally sculpted caverns in the reef crest and wall, which are not only breathtaking in their size, they are also magical as you descend into the gloom before emerging into the azure blue of the outer reef wall. There are so many fish here that the water almost shimmers with their reflected light. Reef hooks are perfect for hanging like a kite in the breeze to watch the big sharks cruise by. The dive boat captains all know the strength of the current and the places where you can be picked up when you eventually have to let go as your air runs out. It's incredibly easy to fall in love with this dive site.

Lake dives

Jellyfish Lake is the other great attraction here; it is one of around 50 lakes located in the central Rock Islands. Some of these are freshwater, others brackish, and some are quite clearly linked to the sea as sharks can be found feeding in them. There are five lakes that have jellyfish, while others have flatworms, shrimp, and a curious horned sea cucumber. Jellyfish Lake on Eil Malk island is home to hundreds of thousands of *Mastigias* jellyfish, one of two species found here. The jellyfish move across the lake to follow the sun as it moves during the day, allowing algae to grow within their bodies which are then absorbed. The lake is reached by a hike through the jungle, so strong boots are a must, but since you will only be snorkeling here, there is no need to lug heavy diving equipment.

Wreck diving

There are also a handful of excellent wrecks off the northern Rock Islands, all casualties of the Second World War. The Japanese wrecks and aircraft are all excellent and well encrusted with marine life, making perfect backdrops for photography. Chandelier Cave is another must for divers who can come up into the air chamber and then chat while swimming among the stalactites that project down from above.

Yap

This island is world famous for its large population of manta rays (*Manta birostris*) and, depending on the time of year, the mantas will congregate in either the eastern or western channels into the main lagoon where they feed on the plankton-rich water that passes through twice daily with the tide.

Diving on the east coast is mainly restricted to the **Goofneuw Channel** between June and October where the manta schools migrate due to prevailing weather conditions and the annual plankton blooms, which feed the reefs. Large packs of grey reef sharks (*Carcharhinus amblyrhynchos*) inhabit the inner lagoon region, as well as blacktip and whitetip sharks. Hawksbill turtles breed on the more secluded beaches here and they will be seen on most dives. There is a large hard coral mound in 40ft (12m) in the channel where the mantas congregate to be cleaned. Slack water after the incoming high tide is always the best time as the visibility will get to around 80ft (25m). Large starry pufferfish (*Arothron stellatus*) can be found "sleeping" on the sand patches and garden eels will be everywhere. Various shells and hermit

Fact file Micronesia

BEST TIME TO GO
Palau has a tropical climate and you should expect heavy rainfall at any time of the year, although December through March are considered the most favorable for diving. Palau is outside the main typhoon zone. Diving in Yap is available throughout the year and there are always mantas to swim with. While there is more rain at the beginning of the year, you should expect it at any time. Chuuk's wet season is December to March while the dry season is May to October, but diving is generally good at any time of the year.

UNDERWATER VISIBILITY AND TEMPERATURE
Visibility in Palau is usually well in excess of 100ft (30m) but it is sometimes difficult to judge because it is just so clear. Water temperatures are fairly stable at around 79–82°F (26–28°C). The visibility in Yap varies in the channels and it is best to dive on the incoming tide when the water is clearest at around 50–80ft (15–25m). Sea temperature is usually around 81°F (27°C). Expect visibility in Chuuk to vary from 60–100ft (18–30m), with temperatures of around 77–86°F (25–30°C).

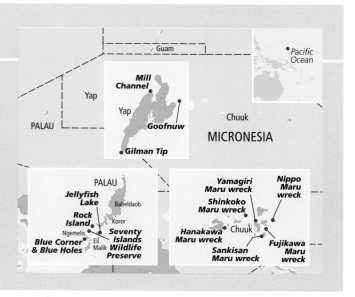

crabs are always around and the usual array of shrimp gobies will attract your attention.

From December through to mid-April, the pack of manta rays migrates back to **Miil Channel** in the northwest of the island, where active mating is usually observed. Most divers hang out in the channel just to watch the large numbers of cavorting mantas as both males and females engage in the acrobatic display. There are a number of cleaning stations in the channel and if you position yourself in the lee of one of these large coral "bommies," you will be treated to an almost neverending procession of mantas as they queue up to be cleaned of parasites by large populations of wrasse and some juvenile angelfish.

All Yap's inner lagoons have healthy mangrove forests which are fed by both saltwater and freshwater runoff from the mountainous interior. The

ABOVE: Huge manta rays are regularly seen in the channels along which the current sweeps, as well as a multitude of sharks, other rays, and tropical fish.

mangroves provide the perfect habitat for juvenile fish and the provision of nutrients that produce the planktonic growth upon which the mantas feed. The southwestern reefs leading down to **Gilman Tip** at the bottom of the island are home to a fantastic array of corals including huge yellow cabbage corals, plate corals, and table corals all stretching out to catch the nutrients in the current. There are huge concentrations of soft corals as well as plenty of crinoids, and if you look closely at these you should be able to spot their commensal shrimp and crabs.

Gilman Tip sits at a natural confluence of two currents, which inevitably attracts large schools of barracuda, jacks, eagle rays, and sharks. Needlefish inhabit the shallows and brilliant red bigeyes and other snapper and grunt can be found in small groups everywhere. Pilot whales have also been seen here. This reef tip is around 2 miles (3km) offshore and is one of the favorite sites for many divers.

All the diving on Yap is done by boat with local guides, as each reef belongs to a particular village or tribe and special permission to dive always has to be obtained beforehand out of respect to them.

Chuuk

Located to the southeast of Guam and Yap is Chuuk. Everyone recognizes that the main attraction here is diving on the sunken Japanese fleet that went to the bottom in the reprisal attack for Pearl Harbor during the Second World War. The remains of around 50 Japanese ships and many warplanes lie mainly around the islands of Fefan, Tonoas, and Uman in Chuuk Lagoon. The raid by American torpedo bombers in 1944 on this important Japanese naval base was so devastating that the Japanese were unable to offer any resistance and the fleet was devastated. Just as swiftly, the Americans moved on and left the islands and their survivors to fend for themselves before the atomic bombs on Hiroshima and Nagasaki brought an end to the conflict.

Chuuk Lagoon has over 140 miles (225km) of outer barrier reef with numerous small islands in the center. The remnants of a once huge mountain, it is around these islands that the sunken Japanese fleet can be found. The depth in the lagoon is quite restrictive for a number of the wrecks, resulting in long surface intervals between dives. While the wrecks get all the attention, there are more than 500 species of soft and hard corals and over 700 species of fish to be enjoyed in the lagoon too. There is now over 70 years of coral growth on the wrecks, making them a photographer's delight.

OPPOSITE: Aircraft shot down during the Second World War are an interesting change from the usual shipwrecks. Most are in shallow water and all are well encrusted with marine growth. The ferocious battles around these islands resulted in catastrophic losses to both sides in the conflict.

Most divers visit Chuuk on a live-aboard dive boat to allow for the best exploration of the wrecks and reefs with the minimum of hassle. At the top of the divers' list is usually the 500ft- (152m-) long freighter *Shinkoku Maru*. Most will do at least two dives on this ship that demands a maximum depth of 130ft (40m). The bow is fantastic with very photogenic soft and hard corals and myriads of tiny damselfish and chromis in the water column. Large dogtooth tuna, jacks, trevally, and barracuda are always around, as well as red coral grouper, sweetlips, and plenty of parrotfish and wrasse feeding on the corals and algae that cover the superstructure.

Other wreck dives

Less frequently visited, the *Hanakawa Maru* has fantastic coral growth on her superstructure which rises from the stern at 110ft (33m) to just below the surface. Her forward hold is still full of old fuel drums, but the interior is very silty and care should be taken with your buoyancy at all times. The *Yamagiri Maru* has the largest artillery shells ever made still stored in her hold. The blown-up *Sankisan Maru* has truck chassis and be sure to check out the guns and tanks on the *Nippo Maru*. She lies between 60–145ft (18–44m) and visibility can be exceptional here. The double-handled telegraph in the bridge is worth looking out for, as are the brilliant white gorgonian sea fans. Surrounded by hordes of glassy sweepers, the soft corals around the coral-encrusted bridge and cabins are breathtaking. Her interior, though silty, has a fantastic array of objects lying around including the galley, medical chests, sake bottles, etc.

The *Fujikawa Maru* is another of those "must dives" with her bow and stern guns covered in corals. She is fairly shallow at between 30–112ft (9–34m). Sitting upright her holds contain airplane parts and an intact Mitsubishi A6M Zero fuselage. It is difficult to decide what to shoot when you photograph these ships, as the wide angle perspective is always tempting, but the amount of macro marine life is simply staggering. If you haven't yet done any specific macro photography dives, this wreck will give you the chance. It has tons of anemones attended by tiny purple shrimp, numerous commensal crabs, and at least four different species of clownfish. Her galley and tiled bathrooms are always popular, but the encrusting marine life on these wrecks is a rare and enjoyable sight. Between Chuuk and Pohnpei to the east are a large number of true coral atolls that are virtually undived by anyone and ripe for exploration.

French Polynesia

Pacific Ocean

Northeast of New Zealand can be found the massive island nation of French Polynesia. It comprises five main island groups: the Society Islands, where the main island Tahiti is found, the Tuamotus, the Marquesas, the Austral group, and the Gambier archipelago. All of the island groups are incredibly scenic. The Tuamotus are particularly stunning. They consist of a massive series of coral atolls where virtually no diving ever takes place, except from a passing private yacht. Once referred to as the Dangerous Islands, this group is exquisite.

Tahiti

French Polynesia is usually referred to simply by the name of its main island Tahiti. This island is the largest in the group and is actually two separate halves joined by a very narrow isthmus. Tahiti Iti to the southeast has vertical walls, topped with lovely *Acropora* corals. The corals are all in very good condition and the barrier reef that runs around the islands is for the most part underdived. There are whale watching excursions here from September through to December, but the main focus is on the diving. You will always find blacktip reef sharks (*Carcharhinus melanopterus*) around the south island. There are some nice stands of black coral and wire corals as well as plenty of large anemones with clownfish and damselfish on them. Bigeye, squirrelfish, small grouper, surgeonfish, and a wide range of butterflyfish are all common, but it is the majesty of the wall and the presence of sharks that is the big draw here.

Tahiti Nui

On Tahiti Nui to the northwest, there are a couple of popular dive sites at the **Aquarium** and **The Wrecks**. The Aquarium is a shallow reef filled with tropical corals and fish. Depth is only around 40ft (12m) so it is perfect for all levels of diver. The Wrecks, near the end of the airport runway, is in a sheltered part of the lagoon which opens out onto the reef wall. An old wooden cargo ship lies on her starboard side at 45° with all of her ribs exposed. Covered in small soft corals and cup corals, some large barracuda hang out in the area as well as coral grouper and lionfish which prey on the millions of glassy sweepers that inhabit the lower areas. Nearby is the wreckage of a Catalina flying boat which was scuttled in 1964. Although there is little marine growth on her fuselage, this is still an interesting addition to the dive. Depth here is around 60ft (18m) and there are plenty of tropical fish everywhere to grab your attention.

Bora Bora

Over on Bora Bora, the action is really all about the manta rays which come through the main channel past one of the piers. Diving with them is always a thrill. Moorea, Bora Bora, and Manihi all offer some shark feeding dives for those who prefer a bit more adrenalin in their life. Stingray dives are also popular on Moorea and this is in 30ft (9m). While perhaps not as spectacular in standard as Stingray City in the Cayman Islands, it is still very enjoyable.

Tahaa and Raiatia are also well worth visiting. As always, it is advisable to dive the passes on an incoming tide. On an outgoing tide the visibility may be very poor and, just at the edge of your vision, you may see reef sharks flashing by to attack the schools of fish caught in the current. Raiatia also has a great wreck called the **Nordby** which is located directly in front of the Hémisphère Sub Plongée dive store in the capital of the island Uturoa.

North in the Tuamotus can be found the atoll of Fakarava which has a massive pass into its lagoon that is over 4,900ft (1,500m) wide. First crossed by the author Robert Louis Stevenson when he was traveling in French Polynesia in 1888, the island pass is famous for its large pelagics with schools of grey reef sharks, manta rays, eagle rays, turtles, and

OPPOSITE: Divers get great opportunities to dive with oceanic silvertip sharks in the channels leading into the lagoons. These encounters are always enthralling.

"... it is the majesty of the wall and the presence of sharks that is the big draw here."

countless fish. The reef to the right of the pass has a large coral plateau and is favored by silvertip sharks, jacks, pompano, bigeye, and hatchetfish. Whitetip reef sharks are also common around the smaller *motu* (or islet), usually seen resting on the rubble bottom.

Most divers want to visit the legendary Rangiroa Atoll, which is one of the largest atolls in the world. Tiputa Pass is a strait in the northwest portion of Rangiroa lagoon joining the lagoon to the open ocean. It leads into the inner lagoon to a small *motu* called Nuhi Nuhi. Starting the dive out on the coral platform to the east of the pass entrance, you will be enthralled by the large schools of bigeye and various snapper. Bottlenose dolphins hang around at the entrance as the incoming tide starts to pull you into the pass. Deep below there are hundreds of grey reef sharks feeding on the fish in the current. Mantas pass by underneath and gradually the pass grows shallow, rising to around 20ft (6m) at the *motu*. Visibility has about halved by this time, but toward the end of the dive, you can enjoy some off-gas time admiring the small soft corals, anemones, clams, and colorful reef fish.

Rurutu

In the southern Austral group is the island of Rurutu. Vaguely shaped like the continent of Africa, it is a focus for humpback whales which come here to calve and mate over three or four months from July to October each year. Off the east and southeast coast of the island, the waters are favorable for this activity and you can take advantage of local knowledge and actually snorkel with these incredible cetaceans. Sightseeing boats are limited to only six passengers, plus a guide and boat captain, and the encounters are by snorkeling only. You will see remarkable whale behavior including spy-hopping, tail and fin slapping, breaching, and general frolicking fun as you struggle to keep up with them. That first plunge into the water, and the sensation of the song of the singing humpback vibrating in your chest, will stay with you forever.

ABOVE RIGHT: Humpback whales congregate around Rurutu from July to October to mate and calve. The males' song travels for hundreds of miles underwater and will reverberate in your chest when you are in the water.

RIGHT: While our attention often focuses on the large encounters, the reefs of French Polynesia are also of excellent quality with a wealth of superb soft corals.

Fact file French Polynesia

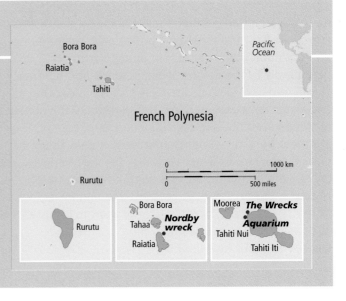

BEST TIME TO GO
July to October is best for the humpback whales around Rurutu. Wet season is November to April with February and March being the hottest and most humid.

UNDERWATER VISIBILITY AND TEMPERATURE
Water temperature is fairly stable at 72–75°F (22–24°C) in the south, but in the Tuamotus in the north where Rangiroa and Fakarava are located it averages from 79–84°F (26–29°C). Visibility is usually in excess of 100ft (30m) except when you get the tide wrong and dive the channels on an outgoing tide—then the "vis" will only be around 17ft (5m) if you are lucky.

Bora Bora
Raiatia
Tahiti

Pacific Ocean

French Polynesia

Rurutu

0   1000 km
0   500 miles

Rurutu

Bora Bora
Tahaa *Nordby wreck*
Raiatia

Moorea *The Wrecks*
Aquarium
Tahiti Nui
Tahiti Iti

Eastern Australia

Southern Pacific Ocean

It is difficult to comprehend the sheer enormity of Australia's **Great Barrier Reef** (GBR). It stretches some 1,430 miles (2,300km) from Lady Elliot Island which lies northeast of the city of Bundaberg in the south, offshore along the entire state of Queensland, past the Great Detached Reef, Raine Island to the top of Cape York, then past Bramble Cay and Black Rock in the Torres Straits. (Although off limits to casual visitors there are thousands of nesting green sea turtles on Raine Island with a record of over 16,000 on one night.) This reef actually continues onward to Papua New Guinea and traverses the western fields of the Coral Sea. This incredible natural phenomenon is home to more than 400 species of coral, 2,000 varieties of fish, 4,000 types of mollusk, not to mention thousands of other invertebrates, vertebrates, and mammals. There are also sea snakes, marine crocodiles, whales, dolphins, and dugong to be found here, while six of the seven species of marine turtles are known to nest among her protected coral cays.

The Great Barrier Reef

It is often described as having the best diving in the world, which is probably due to the range of habitats, scale of the region, and sizes of the reefs. Visibility is not always picture perfect, mainly because the GBR is surrounded for the most part by flat and uninteresting sandy planes which get stirred up regularly and periodically by the innumerable cyclones and storms. These reefs are also susceptible to coral bleaching as sea water temperature rises, the ravages of the crown of thorns starfish, and man's influence, of course. For the most part, the Great Barrier Reef is easy to get to and so many tourists get their first taste of tropical diving here on one of the day boats that operate out of Cairns or Port Douglas. It is exciting and incredible for first-time divers, but if you really want to explore out past Lizard Island and into the Coral Sea, you have to travel by live-aboard.

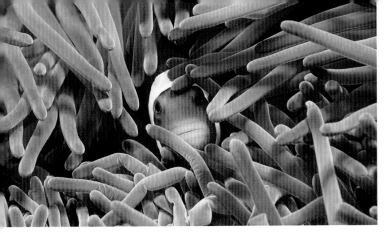

LEFT: Every anemone that you come across will have its attendant anemonefish, which darts back into the confines of the tentacles for protection when danger threatens.
BELOW: The scale of the Great Barrier Reef is simply breathtaking. It supports more than 400 different species of coral and virtually everything else in between.

There are a number of different regions and habitats along the GBR including **Capricorn** and **Bunker Islands** in the south, the Whitsunday Islands, Townsville and Magnetic Island, Cairns and Port Douglas for the **Ribbon Reefs**, the Far Northern Reefs, and the Torres Straits way north toward Papua New Guinea. Primarily the reefs are described as fringing reefs; there are no true coral atolls within the GBR.

The reefs and islands are undoubtedly phenomenal and the challenge that everyone faces is to try and get just a feel for the place and its complexity. Small coral bommies (from the Aboriginal word bombora, which means hidden or dangerous rocks) are like an oasis in the desert and are great places to find concentrations of marine life. Shipwrecks are another consideration and any ship that has been underwater for more than 75 years has automatic protection from the Australian government.

Agincourt Reef in the Ribbon Reefs has a number of great reef dives and **Pixie's Pinnacle** nearby is always popular. It is usually best done at night as the colors really stand out then. There are a great selection of large red anemones and clownfish, large coral grouper, and a myriad of tropical reef fish. **Cod Hole** to the north is justifiably famous. You will find huge potato cod on many dives, and these friendly fish can be particularly "in your face" as they are used to being fed by divers. At only 65ft (20m) deep, you will have plenty of time for this unique interaction.

LEFT: Large potato cod are great fun at the legendary Cod Hole dive site. These large friendly grouper almost become a nuisance to the diver because they are so curious.

Fact file Eastern Australia

BEST TIME TO GO
Diving is available all year round but the months of November to March are considered better overall. Live-aboards also ply the northern reefs during this period.

UNDERWATER VISIBILITY AND TEMPERATURE
Visibility is incredibly variable and for the most part during general GBR reef diving is only around 30–40ft (9–12m). Conditions up in the Coral Sea are better and visibility rises to easily over 100ft (30m). The temperature varies drastically along the coast as it is much cooler in the southern reefs dropping as low as 68°F (20°C) in July and August and rising to 82°F (28°C) in December. Temperatures in the Coral Sea are more stable at around 82–86°F (28–30°C).

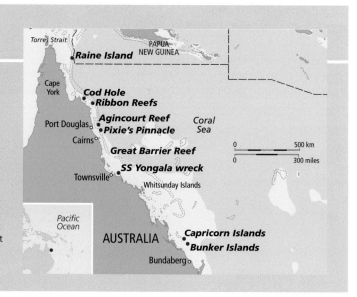

The **SS Yongala** to the south of the Barrier Reef and 15 miles (24km) east of Cape Bowling Green, south of Townsville, is perhaps the wreck that most divers want to see. Located in a very exposed position, unfortunately the dive isn't always possible, but when conditions are right, the wreck is perfect. Lost during a cyclone in 1911, nothing was known of her fate until 47 years later when she was found by accident resting on her starboard side. You descend by mooring line as there is usually a current running on every dive. However, there are always sheltered spots from which to observe massive schools of fish, groups of stingrays, mantas, and even whales and dolphins. Virtually every pelagic species appears to swim by this natural oasis set in the sandy plain at the end of the main channel into the more protected inner lagoon area. Brilliant purple sea fans jostle for

ABOVE: While you are not allowed into the interior of the Yongala, the exterior will more than satisfy your wildest dreams. This vessel really lives up to its status as one of the top shipwrecks, with tons of fish on every dive.

space among small brain corals, lettuce corals, and oysters. Penetration of the hull is not allowed anymore as the interior is regarded as being quite unsafe. However, you will be more than happy with the time spent exploring the exterior of the ship and all of her marine mysteries. The sheer wealth of marine life to be found on this oasis is staggering, particularly for the different species of snapper, grunt, and wrasse. Shoals of stingrays are everywhere, as are the usual attendant huge grouper vying for attention.

New Zealand

Southern Pacific Ocean

It is only possible to include a taste of what New Zealand has to offer as the country is so vast with her two main islands spanning some of the Southern Ocean. South Island has fjords akin to those in Norway with sheltered bays and plunging reefs covered in deep, cold water gorgonian sea fans. Exotically colored wrasse and crustaceans are everywhere. If you can take the time to travel this far, generally the rewards are well worth the effort.

Rainbow Warrior

North Island's main claim to diving fame is the sinking by the French Secret Service of the Greenpeace ship **Rainbow Warrior** in Auckland Harbour in 1985. Sadly one person died on the ship and the ensuing scandal resulted in the resignation of the French Defense Minister. The ship was raised for forensic examination and deemed irreparable; she was then taken to Matauri Bay near the Cavalli Islands where in 1987 she was allowed to sink once more and become a diving attraction and fish sanctuary. The *Rainbow Warrior* is now heavily encrusted with beautiful jewel anemones and the usual leatherjackets, snapper, and damselfish are all around. Moray eels are common as are scorpionfish and spiny lobsters or crayfish. At 131ft (40m) long and in 90ft (27m) of water, the ship is perfect for exploration and most divers will take the trip several times.

Poor Knights Islands

North toward Whangarei and located 14 miles (22km) offshore between Bream Head and Cape Brett, the Poor Knights Islands are a national marine reserve and pending World Heritage Site. They received full protection in 1998 and no one is allowed to fish within 0.5 miles (800m) of them. One of the favorite dives of Jacques Cousteau, they are undoubtedly the focus for all the east coast diving. Due to the mixture of warm water and cold water currents, both subtropical and temperate marine life coexist here. There are around 125 species of fish living amid kelp forests mixed with super colorful anemones,

OPPOSITE In crystal clear water, brilliant cup corals, colorful pincushion starfish, wrasse, and thousands of other exotic marine creatures cover the cavern walls.

gorgonian sea fans, soft corals, encrusting sponges, and resident stingrays which are always passing through this simply massive underwater cavern beneath such an impressive natural arch.

The East Auckland Current originates off the more tropical eastern Australian coastline, passes Lord Howe Island in the Tasman Sea, and then turns southwest to pass through the Poor Knights. The spotted black grouper, yellow-banded perch, and banded coral shrimp are all found here, settled in among resident populations of more temperate species, such as rainbow fish, elegant wrasse, and blue-headed wrasse.

The rugged coastline and offshore islands are packed with marine life and because they jut out into the prevailing current, they are a natural focus for larger pelagic fish as well as a myriad of little critters too. Four species of turtle are recorded from these waters including the loggerhead turtle and the green and hawksbill turtles. Although much rarer, the olive ridley turtle has also been seen here. Large tuna, barracuda, and sailfish as well as a handful of cetaceans including humpback whales are also recorded from the vicinity. Two highlights in the Poor Knights are the Southern Archway, the largest natural arch in the southern hemisphere, and **Rikoriko Cave**, the largest sea cave in the world. As you can imagine, the diving is awe-inspiring as the light filters through the kelp and shoals of tropical fish in water which often has visibility of up to 115–130ft (35–40m). More than anything else, it is the colors of the marine life that are the most striking, as you would normally associate such vibrant colors with tropical waters. This marine park is very much in a temperate zone and it is important to remember that color, diversity, and grandeur isn't limited to warm waters.

Fact file New Zealand

BEST TIME TO GO
Diving is available all year round, but the months of May through to September will see the larger congregations of stingrays which come under the Southern Archway to mate.

UNDERWATER VISIBILITY AND TEMPERATURE
From May to September, during the New Zealand winter, the temperature drops to 57–61°F (14–16°C) but the water is always much clearer at around 60–100ft (18–30m). From September to January, the "vis" can drop to 20–40ft (6–12m), but there are plenty of fish. By February to April, the visibility is back up to around 70ft (21m) and the temperature is between 68–73°F (20–23°C).

Pacific Ocean

see inset

NEW ZEALAND

North Island

South Island

Matauri Bay

Rainbow Warrior wreck

Rikoriko Cave

Whangarei

Poor Knights Islands

Auckland

0   500 km
0   300 miles

Golden Triangle

Eastern Pacific Ocean

The three isolated, offshore island groups of the Galápagos, Malpelo, and Cocos are a natural focus for marine life in an otherwise featureless stretch of the eastern Pacific Ocean. They attract divers from all over the world who are after the ultimate thrill of diving with hundreds of hammerheads, whale sharks, tuna, eagle rays, and sea lions.

The Galápagos archipelago or Archipelago de Colon has been geographically isolated for so long that certain endemic species (as Charles Darwin observed) developed specifically according to the living conditions and environmental factors that they experienced here.

The Galápagos comprise some 20 islands and over 70 islets and span the equator. The cold waters of the Humboldt or Peru Current can register as low as 50°F (10°C), but there are also warm water currents and these are responsible for the curious mix of both warm and cold water species that live alongside each other. These waters provide a safe refuge for many species that are not found anywhere else on the planet. The currents also bring in tons of planktonic nutrients which are the obvious focus for the marine life around the islands.

Volcanic pinnacles

Malpelo and Cocos further to the northeast are isolated seamounts rising from cold, deep water. This means that there is poor coral growth, but huge concentrations of fish. Malpelo belongs to Colombia and is located 305 miles (490km) west of Buenaventura. This jagged group of pinnacles is uninhabited except for a small military outpost which is there to deter illegal fishing in this National Park. The Cocos group lies 300 miles (480km) southwest of Cabo Blanco on mainland Costa Rica. This is another isolated group of volcanic pinnacles which rise up from the depths. Travel time from the mainland is around 36 hours, giving you plenty of opportunity to make new friends and rest before the action begins when you arrive at the islands. Only visited by live-aboard

LEFT: Eagle rays are common hunters around the inshore bays of the Galápagos Islands, feeding on bivalves, crustaceans, and burrowing sea urchins.

BELOW: Be prepared for simply massive schools of fish that congregate at the confluence of the currents. These encounters are the norm here in the Galápagos.

dive boat, the Cocos islands are largely untouched by humans and the tropical rainforest is so spectacular that it was featured in the movie *Jurassic Park*.

All these regions are protected marine heritage sites and are located in tropical latitudes, but due to the great depth around the islands and the predominant tidal streams, they are all fueled by deep cold water upwellings. Surface temperatures are warm, but the colder thermoclines carry nutrient-rich water which encourages the beginning of a complex food chain starting with the smallest phytoplankton and stretching up to the largest pelagic fish and mammals found on the planet.

Galápagos

To the northwest of the main group in the archipelago are the remote islands of Darwin and Wolf. Landing is permitted on Wolf and Darwin—indeed, land tours are a big part of any Galápagos itinerary as tourists can get close to iguanas, penguins, tortoises, turtles, and sea lions as well as numerous species of birds. The research centers are also well worth a visit as they provide a greater insight into the complexity of the creatures which have evolved on the islands.

There are superb dives around Gordon Rocks, North Seymour, Floreana, and Cousins Rocks. **Gordon Rocks** to the east of Santa Cruz Island have depths between 33–130ft (10–40m) and consist of two gigantic lumps of rock which rise from the deep creating weird unpredictable currents in the valley between the rock faces. There are always plenty of snapper, jacks, and turtles as well as various rays passing through and feeding in the nutrient-rich current. North Seymour Island is often favored by divers who want a breather from some of the more punishing strong-current dives. There are good concentrations of fish and a great variety of marine life here, as well as the chance to see stingrays, moray eels, and sea lions.

Floreana island to the south of Santa Cruz has a couple of good dive sites at the north of the island called **Devil's Crown** and **Champion Island**; both are well known for the quality and diversity of marine life including large numbers of moray eels, frogfish, and stingrays. **Cousins Rock** is a rocky ridge to the north of Bartolomé Island and east of Santiago Island. It is only 30ft (9m) in height but around 300ft (90m) long and is home to sea lions, various sharks, and eagle rays. However, it is around Wolf and Darwin that some of the best diving can be found. Not only are the islands breathtaking in their structure, they are simply awesome underwater. It is here that you will find the schools of hammerheads and other shark sightings that are almost legendary.

ABOVE: Turtles are always a good indicator of clear water, abundant marine life, and safe nesting beaches, increasingly rare sanctuaries far away from man's influence.

OPPOSITE: Whale sharks are just one of the many attractions around these isolated seamounts. You may also expect to see eagle rays and schools of hammerhead sharks.

Cocos

There are around 20 dive sites around the main island of Cocos and her satellite pinnacles, with depths quickly dropping to over 130ft (40m). More average diving depths are between 60–100ft (18–30m). There are sheltered bays where you can night dive, but the drift diving and large animal encounters are what divers usually come for.

Fact file Golden Triangle

BEST TIME TO GO
Scuba diving is good all year round, but best between December and April. May to November is hotter (and wetter) but you stand more chance of seeing whale sharks and big schools of hammerheads.

UNDERWATER VISIBILITY AND TEMPERATURE
Although the Galápagos Islands straddle the equator, the water temperature is more temperate due to the massive cold water upwellings from the Humboldt Current. The temperature ranges from 68–77°F (20–25°C) and underwater visibility averages in the 30–80ft (10–25m) range.

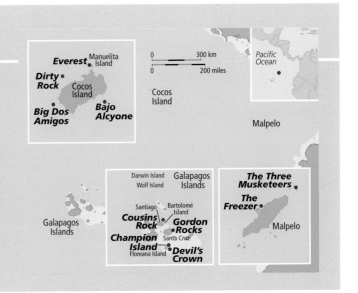

Probably the top site is **Bajo Alcyone** where hundreds of hammerhead sharks can be found as well as other huge schools of big fish. When descending to the submerged seamount 80ft (25m) below you, you will probably see manta and *Mobula* rays as well as several species of shark and jacks. **Dirty Rock** also has great large animal action and is favored by those who are challenged by strong currents. The boulders and pinnacle here form small natural refuges from the current, yet you are still in the middle of the action waiting for that whale shark to come in a little closer.

Manuelita island to the north-northeast is well known for its large numbers of marbled rays and whitetip reef sharks. **Big Dos Amigos** off Punta Rodriguez has an impressive archway at 45ft (14m) as well as pinnacles and canyons where snapper, jacks, sharks, and rays congregate at the cleaning stations. Perhaps the peak, figuratively speaking, is the site known as **Everest** which is reached by submersible from one of the specialist live-aboard dive boats. At depths over 300ft (90m) you will be in the midst of a deep-sea experience that you are unlikely to have witnessed before.

Malpelo

This island is isolated in the Pacific, west of Colombia's Pacific coast and about 225 miles (360km) south of the coast of Panama. Malpelo itself is a big rock with a number of smaller satellites. The island belongs to Colombia and is uninhabited, except for a small military post manned by Colombian army and navy personnel. The island is a national park and a 20-mile (32km) zone around the island has been declared a no fishing zone. In 2006 UNESCO declared Malpelo a World Heritage Site. It is the most barren of all the islands in the Golden Triangle because of its volcanic history and is described as being a portion of oceanic crust. There are no lush tropical rainforests here, only small lichens and ferns which are nourished by seabird guano. But the true beauty of Malpelo lies beneath the waves. Many currents collide around the island, and they bring in a lot of marine life. A huge abundance of fish can be found all around the island, but Malpelo is probably best known for the schooling hammerhead sharks and other large pelagics that congregate there all year.

Malpelo, like all the other oceanic islands, is made up of several islets and rocky pinnacles. Isla Montuosa in the Coiba group, part of Panama's Coiba National Park, is usually visited on the boat trip to Malpelo, just to allow you to get into the water and used to all your equipment in an easier diving environment before you get to Malpelo and dive in its strong currents amid massive shoals of fish.

The diving conditions at Malpelo are very similar to those at Cocos with strong currents off exposed headlands and around offshore pinnacles and seamounts. Many of the dives will feature hundreds of moray eels in the crevices, as well as whitetip reef sharks, snapper, grouper, eagle rays, and *Mobula*

rays. Scalloped hammerheads are always on the list and you will find them on a number of dives in season. The **Three Musketeers**, a group of pinnacles to the south, have a number of swimthroughs, tunnels, and caverns to explore where snapper, soldierfish, frogfish, and wrasse are found in good numbers. Other species of tropical fish are also found here as well as banded coral shrimp and red night shrimp. A dive site known as the **The Freezer** is popular for

ABOVE: Sea lions revel in the schools of tiny fish which come close to shore to mate and lay their eggs. Easy prey, the seals don't have to work hard to get their dinner.

the sightings of scalloped hammerhead sharks, but is not so popular for the water temperature, as the thermoclines here can drop alarmingly, which the sharks love, but divers tend not to.

Baja California

Northeastern Pacific Ocean

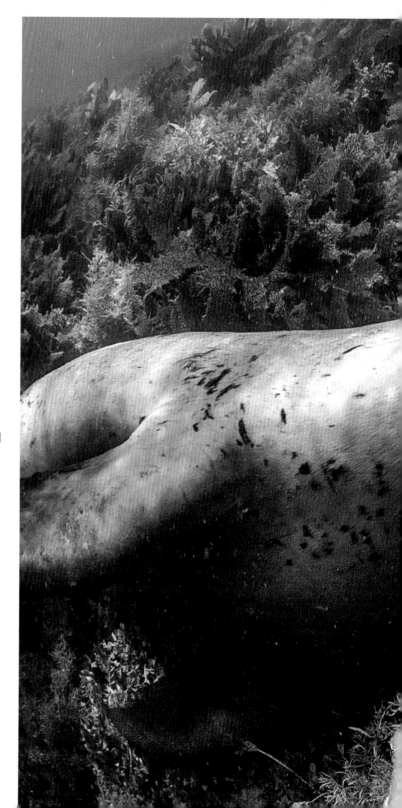

Baja California is a massive peninsula over 1,000 miles (1,600km) long that is located on the western seaboard of North America. It separates the rest of Continental Mexico from the might of the Pacific Ocean and is regarded as one of the most striking geological features on Earth. Probably better known a few years ago for the almost total lack of development and the early heady days of "Hotel California," surfing, and tequila sunrises, Baja has grown into a multicultural province with a number of new resort towns such as Cabo San Lucas at the foot of the peninsula (which sadly looks and feels like just part of California, an American version of what they think Mexico should look like!).

The Sea of Cortez

Usually referred to simply as Baja, the seemingly quiet inland sea between the peninsula and mainland Mexico is called the Sea of Cortez—named after the Spanish explorer who first sighted it. This body of water is home to some of the most exciting marine life encounters found in the world. Migrating blue whales, southern right whales, humpback whales, sailfish, and countless dolphins and other cetaceans all make these waters their home. Sea lions are found aplenty and the variety of marine life in evidence shares a common source with both the Pacific and the Caribbean Sea. The peninsula has a curious geography and features a part-temperate and part-tropical climate. The waters range from the cool conditions of the Pacific with species typically found amid the kelp to warmer waters just a day's drive away where you may be swimming with Indo-Pacific fish such as moorish idols and longnose hawkfish.

La Paz on the east coast is undoubtedly the main center for exploration of the Sea of Cortez and the string of islands to the north of the town include Isla Espiritu Santu, Isla Partida Sur, Isla San Francisco, Isla San Diego, Isla Santa Cruz, Isla San José, Los Islotes, and the El Bajo seamount. Individually outstanding, collectively they form an incredible collection of dive habitats including the wreck of the

BELOW: The sea lions of Los Islotes offer visiting divers some of the most comical and rewarding encounters with any wild animals that you can hope to enjoy.

Salvatierra. This Mexican ferry—a converted US Navy Second World War LST (Landing Ship Tank)—sank in 1976 in only 57ft (17m) of water. There are usually strong tidal currents around her, but these keep the wreck clean and her flanks covered with good quality sea fans and cup corals. Her propeller is smothered in organisms and you should be able to spot longnose butterflyfish (*Forcipiger flavissimus*) and longnose hawkfish (*Oxycirrhites typus*) that are more commonly found in tropical coral reefs.

Los Islotes

Around Los Islotes is one of the largest breeding colonies of Californian sea lions (*Zalophus californianus*) to be found in western Mexico. When you travel to these isolated seamounts, you are likely to be greeted with the sight of a large rookery of sea lions, snoozing, bickering, and playfully diving into the water before hauling themselves back out again to repeat the whole process. As soon as your boat approaches the main rookery, the younger sea lions will dive into the water and swim around the boat, barking at you, enticing you into the water.

Once you enter the water, you'll be quickly surrounded by inquisitive sea lions. Ungainly on land, their speed underwater is quite daunting. The most effective way of photographing them is to sneak up underneath the juveniles as they rest on the surface and compose the shot as a kind of silhouette, with the creature framed basking in the sun, floating upside down on the surface. The shallows next to the shore are also favorable and best explored by snorkeling. There you can swim more freely among the sea lions as they herd fish fry into the shallows

and attack the school from different angles. The excitement of this dive entirely compensates for the lengthy travel time and sometimes rough boat ride needed to enjoy the company of these playful pinnipeds. It certainly merits a place on the list of all divers and snorkelers who visit the region.

El Bajo

Further east are the series of pinnacles called El Bajo. These are covered on all sides by large gorgonian sea fans and sponges, all of which seem to be pulled into curious flattened shapes. The current has a strange countermotion around here and can change direction with no warning. Warmer surface waters mix with the cooler upwelling from the depths to create a curious halocline where the water is hazy as it mixes. The marine life gathers here to feed on the riches that come with the cold water upwellings. El Bajo is one of the world's best dive sites to see schooling hammerhead sharks. It is exhilarating to experience the grace of these curiously shaped sharks which congregate in such vast numbers. These schools range from around six to hundreds of sharks, although such sightings of these shy fish are now rare. While schooling, hammerheads are not aggressive and they generally appear disinterested in divers, which makes them easy to share the waters with.

Cabo Pulmo

This island in the southeast is quite isolated, but well worth the detour en route to Cabo San Lucas or Land's End. Cabo Pulmo has the Sea of Cortez's only coral reef, and although not as brilliant as one would hope, the ancient limestone-forming corals have created a series of ridges that run parallel to the shore in only around 70ft (20m). Brilliant orange and red sea fans can be found in all the nooks and crannies with large numbers of guineafowl puffers, angelfish, snapper, porkfish, moorish idols, and barberfish which, as the name suggests, act as cleaners to the many manta rays that come close into these coral heads. Whale sharks are common and various cetaceans are always spotted traveling close to the shore around here.

LEFT: Baja's sea lions are usually frolicking in the water or sunbathing on the surface, allowing divers a chance to sneak up beneath them and take their photographs in silhouette.
OPPOSITE: Large schools of hammerhead sharks can be found swimming above the El Bajo seamount when tides and currents converge.

Fact file Baja California

BEST TIME TO GO
The warmest waters and kindest seas with clearest visibility are from June to October. Sea lions are found all year round. During November to February, the young pups are at their most playful and inquisitive. With the calmer seas of March and April, the visibility drops around the islands and seamounts, yet this is the best time for sightings of mantas, whale sharks, and whales.

UNDERWATER VISIBILITY AND TEMPERATURE
The temperature is as variable as the visibility! The "vis" can be easily over 100ft (30m) offshore, dropping to only 20ft (6m) when severe currents are running. Temperatures range from 57–79°F (14–26°C) on the Pacific Coast to as low as 57°F (14°C) in the north in the winter months, rising to 91°F (33°C) in the south in the summer.

Channel Islands

Northeastern Pacific Ocean

A number of offshore barrier islands, referred to collectively as the Channel Islands, lie off the southwestern stretch of California. Covering an area of around 348sq miles (900km^2), the eight islands in the group are comprised of San Miguel, Santa Rosa, Santa Cruz, Anacapa, Santa Barbara, Santa Catalina, San Nicolas, and San Clemente. They are part of a National Marine Park and are world renowned for the vibrancy of the kelp forest habitat, and as being home to cavorting sea lions, otters, and many cetaceans.

Guadalupe

The volcanic Guadalupe Island is located 250 miles (400km) southwest of Ensenada in Mexico and 150 miles (240km) west of Isla Cedros and Punta Eugenia. The island is 21 miles (35km) long and 6 miles (9.5km) wide and is inhabited by a handful of fishermen who live in a small camp on the west side. A research team periodically moves onto the island to observe the behavior of the resident population of great white sharks which are, of course, attracted to the large numbers of seals that have made this isolated island their home. Guadalupe Island was formed from two ancient volcanoes and the rugged volcanic ridge rises more than 4,000ft (1,200m) above the sea. Due to its isolated position, it is home to a number of endemic species including the Guadalupe fur seal.

The sharks arrive around the middle or end of July each year and can stay until February. Some tagged individuals have migrated as far as Hawaii and back again. You can only dive from a live-aboard boat and the usual trip lasts for five days with a full day's travel there and back, plus three days in the water. The shark cages are in the water all day. Chumming (see page 98) plays a vital role in attracting the sharks, but once everything is in place, the sharks are quite familiar with the cages and divers are able to get up close and personal with these amazing creatures.

BELOW: Guadalupe Island is world renowned as one of the top three locations for encounters with great white sharks. They appear around August to December each year.

Some live-aboard boats travel back up to the sheltered kelp-filled waters of the Channel Islands National Park as part of the same trip, but most divers either travel out to these northern islands on day boats or choose to stay for long weekends, mainly on Santa Catalina either in the main touristy town of Avalon or in the other small settlement of **Two Harbors**. Two Harbors is best reached by boat and the dive companies will take care of your transport between the two centers. There are a number of offshore rocky spurs, mostly covered by either seabirds or sea lions, and the kelp forest glades are both serene and spectacular with wide avenues, lots of fish and invertebrates, and generally fairly clear, though sometimes cool, water. Diving in dry suits is advisable in the winter months, but good semi-dry suits are more suitable in the summer.

Santa Catalina

Originally settled by Native Americans, Santa Catalina (or Catalina Island) was once owned by the Wrigley family (of chewing gum fame). The picturesque bay filled with small yachts is dominated by a superb Art Nouveau-style rotunda, built (but never used) as a casino. Casino Point Marine Park is the focus for all the shore diving here. There is easy entry down a wide set of steps and you are immediately into the kelp forest. The steeply sloping gravel and sandy seabed is littered with large boulders and mini-walls which act as permanent holdfasts for the kelp. The crevices have California spiny lobster, and most recesses are home to pairs of brilliant orange Garibaldi, a type of damselfish. They often congregate in small groups, but are very aggressive toward divers if you stray too close to their nesting sites. Giant stingrays and even Pacific electric rays (*Torpedo californica*) are common, as are the comical-looking horn sharks (*Heterodontus francisci*). Giant kelp (*Macrocystis pyrifera*) is one of the fastest growing algae on the planet—it can grow over 24in (60cm) in a day, and reach over 200ft (60m) in length. The air-filled bladders keep the leafy blades afloat on the surface and create a canopy that cuts down the natural sunlight filtering through from above, while allowing enough through for marine organisms that love the shade to thrive.

There is very little tidal movement, but although you would think that current movements could be charted, as they are in British waters, that is not the case around Santa Catalina. In my experience of one week's diving in the same area, for about three hours one afternoon the tidal race was extreme, over

4 knots. The kelp forest was pushed flat to the sea bed and it was too dangerous to dive beyond the inshore reef.

A road traverses this very rugged island, running past the tiny airport north to the village of Two Harbors located at the isthmus. If you think you see a small herd of wild buffalo, you are not mistaken. Most passengers take the ride to Two Harbors by boat, as it is much more scenic. To the east of the jetty are a series of small guano-covered rocks called **Ship Rock** and **Bird Rock**. The kelp on the inside of these rocks is very lush and thick and passage through it can be quite difficult, unless you are in one of the many canyons that cut through the seabed to an average depth of about 60ft (18m). The outer wall of Ship Rock drops almost vertically to 120ft (36m) to a sandy seabed. Large salps and jellyfish often get caught in the kelp fronds and there are usually all manner of nudibranchs, small snails, and fish around the forest. Small bluehead gobies, various nudibranchs, and snails are all around the rocky substrate. Various species of rockfish, sheephead, and even sea lions are common here, but most of the sea lions congregate at the southern tip of the island at a clump of boulders called Church Rock.

Church Rock is in an exposed location and is subject to different tidal streams and so the currents here can be quite fierce. Depths are only around 40–60ft (12–18m). Here you can enjoy the best of the kelp forest glades and seek shelter among the huge boulders and mini-walls. Rockfish, sargo, and Garibaldi are all present and if the sea lions are in a playful mood, they will come very close to you.

OPPOSITE: Purple gorgonian sea fans (*Eugorgia rubens*) are found in shallow depths of around 60ft (18m) off the Casino Point Marine Park, much shallower than usual for this species.

ABOVE: Garibaldi are a large brilliant orange species of damselfish. They are friendly and inquisitive, but can become aggressive if you stray too close to their nesting sites.

Fact file Channel Islands

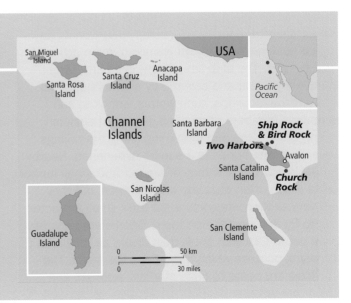

BEST TIME TO GO
Early spring is usually great as the kelp forests are fantastic and there are fewer divers around the Channel Islands. During the summer months, expect lots of tourists—many of the dive sites can be busy with day boats coming over from Long Beach and other Californian coastal towns. August through to October are probably the peak months for diving with great white sharks at Guadalupe Island.

UNDERWATER VISIBILITY AND TEMPERATURE
During the summer months, the visibility will average around 30–60ft (9–18m), but it can easily get as clear as 80ft (25m) in the winter months, after the first of the big storms has cleared away all of the dead and rotting seaweeds. Winter months experience temperatures of around 52°F (11°C), but the dive sites are less crowded and the kelp forests are pristine and lush with the start of the new season's growth. Temperatures can rise to 75°F (24°C) during July and August.

San Miguel Island
Santa Rosa Island
Santa Cruz Island
Anacapa Island
USA
Pacific Ocean
Channel Islands
Santa Barbara Island
San Nicolas Island
Ship Rock & Bird Rock
Two Harbors
Avalon
Santa Catalina Island
Church Rock
San Clemente Island
Guadalupe Island

0   50 km
0   30 miles

Vancouver Island

Northeastern Pacific Ocean

The diving up the entire coast of California, Oregon, and Washington State is spectacular, even although many areas can be blown out by those massive Pacific swells. However, that just directs your attention to Vancouver Island where the diving is predominantly undertaken along the sheltered east coast. Vancouver Island is located in the province of British Columbia in Canada and is the largest Pacific island east of New Zealand. It measures 12,407sq miles (32,134km^2) in area. Jacques Yves Cousteau proclaimed that the spectacular coastal waters of British Columbia, Vancouver Island and Nanaimo (a district on the east coast of the island) are "the best temperate water diving in the world and second only to the Red Sea." The entire region consistently comes top of the list for the best diving in North America.

Most visitors to Vancouver Island arrive by ferry from Horseshoe Bay just north of the city of Vancouver. These mighty ships are always stuffed full of tourists with huge Winnebago camper vans pulling cars and boats, topped with kayaks and dive gear. Taking about 90 minutes to cross the sound, once you arrive at Nanaimo, everyone quickly disperses into an island almost the size of England!

On first arrival, many divers will dive on the **HMCS Saskatchewan**, a former Canadian Navy Coastguard frigate sunk deliberately off Nanaimo as an artificial reef in 1997. The ship lies upright in 112ft (34m) completely intact and covered by anemones, small sea urchins, scallops, tube worms, crinoids, and countless numbers of rockfish. Her main deck is in only 60ft (18m) and swimming along the railings covered in anemones is a superb experience. Nearby Snake Island has a colony of around 250 small harbor seals which often buzz you on the wreck, but they are very skittish when you enter their small protected bay to try and photograph them. Snorkelers generally have better luck with them than divers as they aren't releasing bubbles which may spook the seals. The shallows are home to huge starfish, wolffish, and spider crabs.

Neck Point adjoining the shore north of Nanaimo is one of the best places to find wolf eels. Very similar to its British cousin, the Pacific wolf eel (*Anarrhichthys ocellatus*) is much larger and has a face that only its mother could love! Females and juveniles are a reddish brown in color and mating pairs will be found in the same hole. The wolffish were friendly when I was there and needed no coaxing to get some great photographs. What was more astonishing was the amount of invertebrate life: wherever you looked there were huge nudibranchs, colorful spider crabs, burrowing crabs, red sea urchins, orange sea pens, and a different kind of kelp. In some ways the diving was similar to that in the UK, yet at the same time it was completely different and very rewarding.

Gabriola Island

Over on Gabriola Island, the wall just drops away from the rolling edge at 40ft (12m) and descends in vertical slabs way beyond where you can dive. At 80ft (25m) there are some horizontal ledges which have hundreds of shrimp on them, while the wall itself has thousands of large red anemones, very similar to dahlia anemones. The white-spotted anemone (*Urticina lofotensis*) is particularly colorful and you should be able to see small shrimp around its base, hiding under the tentacles. Tiny sculpin are everywhere and larger rockfish hover nearby to check what you are up to.

Dodd Narrows

Nearby **Dodd Narrows** is a narrow passage that funnels the full might of the tidal stream between Vancouver Island and neighboring Mudge and Gabriola Islands and at full running tide it can reach speeds of over 8 knots. We dived here at slack water down along a tumble of boulders totally smothered with

OPPOSITE: Giant Pacific octopuses are curiously friendly and often interact with divers. Their outstretched tentacles make graceful movements as they swim silently by.

"The best temperate water diving in the world and second only to the Red Sea."

plumose anemones. The undersides were covered with jewel anemones, cup corals, and encrusting sponges, with exotic-looking species of fish of the sculpin family everywhere. These sculpin include fish that look like our common gobies and blennies to scorpionfish. In among them are some rather weird and wonderful exceptions (as there always are) to every rule. The grunt-nosed sculpin (*Rhamphocottus richardsonii*) is only about 3in (10cm) long, has a piglike snout and large pectoral fins with extended fin rays which it uses like feet to hop around the sea bed. It is fairly drab in color with a marbled appearance except for its tail which is bright orange.

This narrow passage was also stuffed with huge sea pens which are found wherever there is a sandy patch. Rockfish are always in evidence and there are also huge aggregations of purple-spined sea urchins and dead man's fingers. After 20 minutes of slack water, the current started to pick up running into the sound and it was prudent to work among the larger boulders and swim into shallower water where huge colonies of aggregating green anemones (*Anthopleura elegantissima*) smothered the shallow rocks at the tide line. Gabriola Pass and Porlier Pass are very similar and equally as entertaining in the current.

ABOVE: Wolffish are usually nocturnal feeders, but they are found regularly on most dives around the coast of Vancouver Island in quite shallow waters.

Port Alberni is the main port of call on the west coast and you must pay a visit to Tofino for whale watching. **Barclay Sound** off Port Alberni is famed for its humpback whales, sixgill sharks, large sea lions, and many shipwrecks. Visibility may not be as good as on the more sheltered east coast, but the diving and the setting are spectacular.

Quadra Island and Seymour Narrows

As you travel north along the east coast of Vancouver Island, one of the first stopping points is **Quadra Island**, near the town of Campbell River. A small ferry ride takes you over to Quadra Island. Diving here is strictly at slack water as these are some of the fastest-moving currents on the planet. Be prepared for early morning and evening dives as part of any trip here. Copper Cliffs in particular are subject to the strong tidal stream and no matter how much you plan and plot and scheme, sometimes the tide will just not go slack. It can change direction at any time when you will see the large stands of bull kelp leaning in another direction or getting pulled underwater. This is a vertical wall to 100ft (30m) before it slopes off steeply into the depth over some huge boulders covered with even larger cloud sponges, quite exotic-looking long tubes in these cold northern waters.

The diving here is done on the periphery of the fabled **Seymour Narrows** which were once described by Captain George Vancouver, who first explored the island, as one of "the vilest stretches of water in the world." The current, even after the removal of Ripple Rock in 1958, has been scientifically measured as being the strongest on the planet. (Ripple Rock was a twin-peaked submerged mountain midway in the channel. Charges totaling 1,375 tons of explosive were used to remove it as it was such a hazard to shipping, resulting in the largest deliberate nonnuclear explosion on Earth.)

The wall here is deeply cut by horizontal fissures where you can see octopuses, shrimp, and lots of nudibranchs. Much of the vertical wall is covered with jewel anemones, very similar to European species, except these are just one color—in Vancouver they are called strawberry anemones (*Corynactis californica*). Spotfin sculpin are particularly brightly colored with red patches and a high dorsal fin, while the snubnosed sculpin (*Orthonopias triacis*) is even more goby-shaped and even more brilliantly splotched! Another couple of striking fish are the painted greenling (*Oxylebius pictus*) with its brilliant red vertical bands and the similarly colored tiger rockfish (*Sebastes nigrocinctus*) which is quite shy.

It is possible to take snorkel and dive trips down Campbell River to watch the migrating salmon heading upstream to their spawning grounds. Further north is Port Hardy where you can be picked up and taken out to the resort of God's Pocket, located a 30-minute boat ride out on Hurst Island. You can also dive to your heart's content off the pontoons and the night diving here always yields octopuses. Giant nudibranchs, sculpin, various little shrimp, and Puget Sound crabs are found in abundance and while the depth is only 40–60ft (12–18m), it is probably the cold water that will limit your time underwater, rather than too much nitrogen in your bloodstream.

Browning Wall at God's Pocket is regarded as one of the best vertical wall dives in temperate waters and is famous for its 100ft (30m) visibility. It is filled with deepwater basket stars, colorful king crabs, rockfish, lingcod, wolf eels, and lots of brilliant red jewel anemones, dahlia anemones, and plumose anemones. Nearby Hunt Rock consists of a couple of submerged pinnacles that are marked by a green mooring buoy. Five Fathom Rock has so many different species of rockfish that the Fisheries and Oceans Administration of Canada designated it a Rockfish Conservation Area in 2007. Other dive sites in the immediate area include Barry Islet, Dillon Rock, One Tree Island, Nakwakto Rapids, and several sites in Bates Pass.

Much of the diving around Vancouver Island is naturally done by boat to get to the best sites, but with a coastline that stretches forever, there are always lots of little sheltered bays and inlets which are perfect for shore diving. The only limiting factor in Vancouver Island is that there are so few access points to get down to the coast.

Fact file Vancouver Island

BEST TIME TO GO
Diving can be done all year round with proper thermal protection. Although dry suits are preferred, 6–7mm wet suits will also work during the summer months. Each season offers something different, with lots of juvenile fish in the spring. Summer brings light winds, some fog, and more consistently clear water. Orcas and humpback whales begin arriving in early May. September and October mean rougher seas and less comfort on the dive boats, but the visibility can be in excess of 200ft (60m).

UNDERWATER VISIBILITY AND TEMPERATURE
Visibility is always variable and when the spring melt water from the mountains comes down into the passes, there may be as much as 10ft (3m) of murky "tea-colored" fresh water on the surface, which you have to swim through to get to the crystal clear water beneath. The water temperature will vary from 42–55°F (6–13°C) during the winter and 53-61°F (12–16°C) during the summer.

Index